Kate Boydell was widowed in 1998 after nine years of marriage to her beloved husband Charlie. Charlie was a fit and healthy 28-year-old when he contracted a virulent bacterial heart infection shortly before their wedding, and had to undergo two bouts of open-heart surgery six weeks later. Despite this initial set back, he and Kate enjoyed nine years of blissful married life. Charlie's tragically early death at the age of 37 followed a long battle with the problems associated with the initial heart surgery. He suffered heart failure at home after a bout of 'flu, and died in Kate's arms, leaving her with two small children to bring up single-handed.

Kate felt compelled to write a book about Charlie, and their life together, and it was the struggle to find a publisher for her first book – *Big-Hearted Man* – that prompted Kate to write an online survival guide for young widows. The success of the website www.merrywidow.me.uk prompted calls from many widowers for a similar guide for men and so Kate decided to write a comprehensive guide to bereavement, offering clear and practical advice for anyone who has lost a partner. *Death . . . And How To Survive It* is the result.

If you have any comments, you can e-mail Kate at merrywidow@boydells.com

D1350117

Death ...
And How To
Survive It

**A unique, practical and uplifting guide
to coming to terms with the loss of your partner**

Kate Boydell

Vermilion
LONDON

3 5 7 9 10 8 6 4 2

First published in the United Kingdom in 2005 by Vermilion, an imprint of Ebury Publishing
Random House UK Ltd
Random House
20 Vauxhall Bridge Road
London SW1V 2SA

Random House Australia (Pty) Limited
20 Alfred Street, Milsons Point, Sydney,
New South Wales 2061, Australia

Random House New Zealand Limited
18 Poland Road, Glenfield,
Auckland 10, New Zealand

Random House (Pty) Limited
Isle of Houghton, Corner of Boundary Road & Carse O'Gowrie
Houghton 2198, South Africa

Random House UK Limited Reg. No. 954009
www.randomhouse.co.uk

Papers used by Vermilion are natural, recyclable products made from wood grown in sustainable forests.

A CIP catalogue record is available for this book from the British Library.

ISBN 9780091902575 (from January 2007)
ISBN 0091902576

Text design by seagulls

Printed and bound in Great Britain by
Mackays of Chatham plc, Chatham, Kent

For Sarah, David, and all the other poor souls journeying out of the darkness and into the light. Walk straight and tall, and know that I walk beside you every step of the way.

contents

Part Two: Out into the Light

acknowledgements

I would like to pay tribute to all the people who have contributed to this book. Thanks to their honesty and candour, I have been able to write an account of bereavement that encompasses the experiences of a wide spectrum of men and women. My thanks go to the following people for their valued contributions, in no particular order: Harriet Knight, Gill Woodman, Richard Martin, Ann Nevard, Tony R., Jennie Leyden, Carolyn Roberts, Christine Myers, Robin Walker, Rebecca Chapman, Josie Arkle and Tracy Jones.

Special mention must go to two friends who are both articulate and voluble on the subject of widowhood. Their intelligent, reasoned contributions to this book have been invaluable, and their friendship is something that I treasure, even though we have never met. Sarah Snaydon and David Robarts provide a constant source of encouragement; they write to me often, and help to provide the critical benchmark on which I base my writing. I am indebted to them for their help with this book.

When I wrote this book I thought it would remain unpublished but, thanks to an appearance on *Radio Five Live*, my prayers for a brave and ballsy publisher were answered. Therefore, my thanks go to Simon Mayo for having me as a guest on his show on *Radio Five Live*, and for giving me sufficient time to talk about death – a subject that is all too often ignored. The radio broadcast was heard by a man called Antony Heller, who went into work the next day and told his colleague to take a look at my website. Antony's colleague, Amanda Hemmings, duly took a look at my website and liked what she saw. If you have found this book helpful and enlightening, then you have Amanda Hemmings, former Editorial Director at Vermilion, to thank for its publication. She saw its possibilities, rescued me from obscurity and gave me the chance to bring my message of hope to a wider audience. I will be forever indebted to her for giving me encouragement and giving me confidence in the validity of my writing. She has championed my work and backed me every step of the way, and it is a great sadness to me that her impending motherhood has brought an end to our working relationship. Amanda, I wish you and your young family every happiness for the future and thank you from the bottom of my heart for having faith in me.

I would also like to thank Charles Wace for providing support for the merrywidow website. He has remained a committed and generous friend, and thanks to his kindness and the hard work of Jim Wilkinson, Owen Wallis and all the staff at Two Four TV.com, many thousands of widows and widowers have gained comfort and hope from reading www.merrywidow.me.uk – the online guide on which this book is based.

Beth Burrell has remained a constant in my life and is, without doubt, the best friend any girl could have. She is the only person outside Vermilion to have read this book prior to publication. I trust her judgement implicitly and owe her a debt I can never repay.

And lastly, I would like to thank my family and friends for all they have done for me over the last six years. This is the first time any of them will have seen the book. I hope they like it and appreciate the fact that it is blissfully free of typos . . .

introduction

Imagine a black whirlpool, dark and powerful, strange and forbidding. Imagine that whirlpool at the end of a hospital bed; imagine it swirling around the receiver of a telephone; imagine looking into the inky vortex and feeling yourself being drawn towards it. You can see it, you know it's there, but you cannot bear to think that you will ever be taken down into its fathomless depths.

But you know you are about to feel it.

Feel it.

Feel those words, 'She's gone', 'He's dead', 'There was nothing more we could do'. Feel yourself being pulled into the blackness. See nothing; hear nothing; feel nothing – nothing except those terrible, terrible words.

Feel each letter burn into your consciousness. Feel the words carbonise. Feel the blackened ashes fall away, leaving behind an everlasting imprint – a scar in your mind and on your heart.

Down you go. Sucked deeper and deeper until hope becomes a tiny speck of light in the far distance. You can see people around you, but their words are lost to you. You are lost.

All hope is lost.

All is blackness.

Nothingness.

Hell.

~

Death. It's a bit depressing, isn't it?

Nobody wants to talk about it.

But I do.

Nobody wants to have a visit from the Grim Reaper. If you are on his list, he will come to your house and take you, or someone you love. It's too depressing to think about. But then death is depressing, and brings us untold misery – which is why he's called the Grim Reaper and not the Happy Shopper.

I had the Grim Reaper in my house. He came to visit one day and left my husband dead on the carpet. He came and took a young father away from his wife and infant daughters. He came and took my love from me, and at the time there was nothing I could do to stop him.

But I can do something now.

I can write about all I have been through and let people know that death does not mean the end of your happiness; that death doesn't mean you are never able to smile again; that death can be beaten.

I want to tell all of those people who have lost a partner in the prime of life that death will give them gifts – gifts that set them apart from others.

Death left me naked. Stripped bare.

I had no protection.

I was shivering and cold and alone.

Death took my shining knight, my suit of armour, my sword and my shield. But what death took was invisible to others. The outside world didn't know about my marital armour. The outside world couldn't see the strength my husband gave me, the confidence he instilled in me, the love that filled me up and made me the vibrant, vital 33-year-old woman that I was.

Death took from me.

But now I have taken from death, and what I have taken I am giving to you.

I'm not going to drone on about all the misery I've been through because you don't want to hear that – the last thing you need right now is to read somebody else's tale of woe. No, I'm going to tell you all the things you won't be able to learn anywhere else.

I'm going to give you a beginner's guide to death.

~

How many people do you know who are in the same position as you? Is there anyone in your street, in your block of flats, in your neighbourhood, who has just lost a partner in the prime of life? Is there anybody in your immediate circle of friends who isn't happily married, or part of a couple?

No?

You're a bit stuck then, aren't you?

Well, not any more.

I've been through what you're going through, and now I'm going to tell you all the things I wish I'd been told when my husband died – things you won't hear from the vicar or the undertaker, from your GP or your counsellor; things that only someone who's had a house call from Mr G. Reaper would know. What you are about to read is a practical guide to bereavement, based on my own experiences and those of men and women like me.

In the summer of 2002 I wrote a survival guide for young widows, and published it on the Internet. The response to www.merrywidow.me.uk was immediate and overwhelming; I had e-mails from all over the world, from men as well as women, telling me that what I had written was unique because it so accurately described their emotions at the time. I wanted more people to have access to this information, and I also wanted to include advice for widowers. This book is the result.

I am not a counsellor or a doctor; I'm not a learned academic and I have no letters after my name. I cannot back up my arguments with anything other than honest reasoning, but I do have one thing in my favour – personal experience. You won't have to visit a self-help group; you won't need drugs or drink to do what I have done. All you will need is an open mind and a little self-belief. I want to tell all those people who feel their life is over that there is hope and a future. You *can* live without your partner. I won't try to tell you that it's going to be easy or quick, but it will be an interesting journey. I'm not a death guru or a philosopher; I can't couch my words in scientific theory or psychobabble.

I'm just an ordinary woman, and I'm going to give it to you straight.

part one

through the darkness

1

when death hits you

I buried my life on 8 April 1998. I buried my husband and my hope. I buried my joy. I buried my love. And there was nobody – nobody to whom I could turn who understood exactly how I felt. I looked for books of poetry; for books on death; for something to tell me how I should be feeling and how the hell I was going to survive. But there was nothing for a woman like me.

People have lots of theories about death, and generally those theories exist to make the people concerned feel better about themselves. After all, it's easier to think that a person isn't suffering too badly than to confront the reality of their situation. You can tell a young widow that she's lucky to have her youth, and that she has plenty of time to meet somebody else, because it's so much easier than comforting her over what she's lost. You can tell a widower that he'll be bound to find a new wife soon, because it's easier than helping him to cope with the everyday struggle of having to bring up a family by himself. People will do almost anything to avoid actually having to confront death and its consequences, but some of us have no choice. The way we face up to it, and the manner in which we conduct ourselves subsequently, will make the difference between peace of mind and perpetual torment.

~

When death hits you, it hits you hard. You feel concussed – as if you have been beaten over and over again until you are too blind, confused and hurt to feel anything anymore. But the beating does not take long. It takes only a second for you to be reduced from a normal, happy individual to a bloody, senseless pulp. And in your head you are screaming, but the person you are trying to reach cannot hear you, cannot see you, cannot touch you any more. Your life is slipping away from you – slipping under a white sheet, slipping into the back of an ambulance, slipping down a gloomy corridor on a stainless steel trolley.

Your life is slipping away.

You feel a sense of unreality – dazed and confused, as if you had been pushed out onto an open stage in front of a packed auditorium. People expect you to say something, to do something, but you are frozen to the spot.

> **Even if you thought you had prepared yourself for this moment, the reality of it will take your breath away.**

So there you stand, under glaring spotlights, with a hushed audience hanging on your every word. And suddenly, a switch is thrown in your head, and your world is plunged into darkness. At a single stroke you have lost your future, your past, your identity and your position in society.

You are numb.

The numbness is not an affliction but a self-preservation measure. It is your brain's way of giving you time to get over the shock of what has happened to you. It is the same mechanism that your brain would employ were you suddenly to have a limb torn off. Your body would not be able to cope with the pain if it were allowed to feel it immediately, and so your mind numbs all feeling until you are better able to cope with it. Losing a limb and losing a partner are much the same; part of you has been torn away but you are able to view the bloody stump that remains with a calm detachment that others might find rather alarming. You are not alarmed because you simply cannot feel anything. Your brain is blocking the understanding of your situation, so that although you can hear the words, 'He's gone' or 'She's dead', you cannot comprehend their true meaning. The words are frozen. Your brain will absorb them, but will only allow them to melt into your understanding when you are sufficiently able to deal with their impact upon you. So you go home, you put the phone down, you go to work, you collect the children from school in a swirling, numbing fog.

~

When I was allowed in to see Charlie's body, I knelt down and held him, and then I felt a great welling up inside me, and I threw back my head and I let out an inhuman, animalistic wail. The widow's wail. It was almost as if my body was allowing one, short burst of emotion to escape me before shutting down totally. It came from deep inside me and seemed to continue long after all the air had left my lungs. And once it had left me, my joy and the capacity to feel love left me too. I felt as if somebody had taken a sledgehammer and hit me square in the chest; I went into shock after a couple of hours and my legs went into involuntary spasm. It was unreal to me; I was detached from it; I had emotional concussion. I felt nothing of myself, but I could still feel the pain of others. I couldn't read nursery rhymes to my baby girl without breaking down. Alice was too small to understand why her mummy was crying; she was unaware that in the room below her lay her dead father, the light gone from his eyes, a picture of her smiling face in his wallet.

But I knew.

'Lavender's green, dilly dilly, lavender's blue.'

I knew.

'When I am king, dilly dilly, you shall be queen.'

I knew.

I kissed her goodnight, and then she slept.

But I could not.

~

So why didn't I feel anything? Why did I feel for Alice and Rosie and yet have no emotional attachment to my own situation? Simple – because if I had any grasp at that moment of the true impact of what had just happened to me, I would have lost it – I would have lost my mind. My love for my husband was so strong and so true that to actually acknowledge his loss would have brought about a complete mental and emotional breakdown.

So I went downstairs and called everyone I could think of to tell them the news. I told my family and Charlie's family. I comforted them and then I went to bed – a mechanical reaction to an emotional catastrophe.

The fog had descended.

telling the children

I will never forget lying awake in the early hours of the morning, waiting for Rosie to wake up. She was only four years old and I knew that what I said to her had to be phrased in such a way that it didn't upset her too much, but at the same time it had to be the truth.

She didn't react as I thought she would. Instead she ran out of the room and woke each family member staying in the house in turn with a cheery, 'My daddy's dead'.

I wish I could tell you that it's not so bad, that telling your children that their father or mother is dead is a relatively painless process because they are young and don't really understand the full implications of what has been said.

But I can't.

> **Telling your children that they have just lost a parent is the hardest thing you will ever have to do.**

Of course you could put off the awful moment. You could tell your children that their daddy has gone away on business for a while, or that mummy is visiting friends, to give yourself a chance to prepare.

Don't do it.

Be truthful to your children from the outset. Tell them everything. Tell them how mummy died, where daddy died, what they died from.

And if you think you can't do it, that you can't cope with the strain of telling them such upsetting news when you yourself feel suicidal with grief, think only of them and not of yourself.

It took Rosie a while to fully comprehend that her daddy was never coming home. Her sister Alice was only 19 months old and so never really questioned his absence. To her 'Daddy's gone to London' and 'Daddy's dead' amounted to the same thing – he wasn't there. Small children have little understanding of the concept of death; they think that daddy or mummy is just away, and that they will walk through the door one day and everything will be all right again. In that respect they will demand enormous patience. You will have to explain to them over and over again. You will have to try to make them understand what is beyond their comprehension. And all the time you will feel like screaming. All the time you will feel like walking out of the house and leaving your children because you can't bear to shoulder their grief and their endless questions and demands for attention when you yourself are being torn apart. But you can't walk out. You have to bear it. You have to support your children and give them love and understanding, even when you feel empty and lonely and insane with your own grief. And if you can bear it, if you can be honest and open right from the start, then at least you will have a chance. At least you will have a chance to make your children happy again.

2

the morning after: tea and sympathy

So you wake up and imagine that it must have been a horrible dream. But it wasn't – it was real, and the horrible dream is just beginning. If you have people staying with you they will be busying themselves with making tea – because tea is what people give you when you've just had a shock. Tea makes it all better. You will be awash with it. When people cannot think of what to do or say, they put the kettle on. It acts as an emotional punctuation mark; it gives them something to do, and it gives you something to occupy your mouth with so that you can stop crying for a moment – only you're not crying; you're wondering how the tea will be able to make its way past the large obstruction occupying the space where your sternum used to be.

What is that thing?

The lump, for want of a better word, is your body's way of preventing the grief exploding out from you. It will sit just above the seat of your emotions, and there it will stay until your mind decides you are sufficiently able to control your grief. The lump will also obstruct any food you try to eat – not that you'll have much appetite. You will regard food with the same bleak disdain as would a ballet dancer or a supermodel. You don't need it – what good will it do you? Food is about pleasure, isn't it? And your pleasure receptors have shut down for the duration.

So you'll struggle to eat your toast and drink your tea. You'll get the children their Coco Pops, and you'll cry into their milk while your back is to them, then you'll put their breakfast in front of them and try to act as if nothing has happened. And all the while those people who are with you to give you support and love will be watching you, waiting for their chance to give you a hug or another cup of tea. But they can't give you back what you really need. They can't give you back your partner or the mother or father of your children; they can't give you the one thing that will make everything all right again. So they give you tea, and you drink the tea and try not to cry, and all the while you are wishing you were sipping from a mug of hemlock.

And then you have to take yourself upstairs and get dressed, and getting dressed will be difficult for a number of reasons. You will be so confused and numb that you will have trouble with any fastenings that present themselves to you. Buttons and zips will appear strange and unfamiliar; socks will be reluctant to embrace your feet; cuffs will not fasten and jumpers will scratch. But his clothes will just fall upon you; his shirt will be comfortable, his sweater will fit you; her blouse will be soft against your skin, just as she was. You will want to wear his clothes; you will want to press her garments close, so close that you absorb the last traces of your dead love into your living flesh. And then you stop. You see yourself holding on to his favourite shirt or clasping her nightdress to your cheek; you see the reflection of a lost love; you see that shirts and jumpers, shoes and skirts are all that you will ever have to hold.

But how they smell.

They still smell, and nobody can take that away from you. That smell is yours and yours alone.

Smell is a living trace of a person and it remains alive when they are not. You will find yourself kneeling by the washing basket, bending over a drawer, spraying perfume on your pyjamas or aftershave into your blouse.

You will want to be close to that smell; you will want to have that smell close to you. You will sleep with his shirt. You will hold on to that shirt so very tightly. You will do it, because clothes and smell and touch are all you have to cling to now.

So cling to them. Fill your head with her scent, walk around in his boxer shorts – do whatever it takes.

And when you are up and dressed you will be ready to begin. The ache in the centre of your chest is starting to throb. More tea? No, you don't want any more tea – you want to put your hand over the spout of the boiling kettle because you know you won't feel any pain. Pain is alien to you now, just as love and light and joy are alien to you. All you know is darkness – swirling, sucking, desolate emptiness. But you are not feeling it yet.

Not yet.

other people

The friends you have told about your partner's death will have told others, and the phone will begin to ring. It will ring throughout the day, and it will continue to ring for days. You will almost certainly want to speak to everybody in person, but it does help to have a close relative on hand to field calls when you don't feel you can talk. At the same time as the phone begins to ring, people will be knocking on your door. For me it became like a conveyor belt of grief: I would welcome the first person of the day into the study; they would cry. I would tell them how Charlie died and that he didn't suffer and that the children were fine. Then I would have to get up and answer another phone call, and then I would say goodbye to my visitor and await the imminent arrival of the next one. It went on like that for days. It was a mark of the respect and love that people had for Charlie, and as Charlie's widow, I knew I had a responsibility to them. So I did my duty, I helped my friends and I quietly prayed that they would return the favour when I needed them.

You should prepare yourself to hear news about your partner's death that has been distorted or sensationalised in some way. When Charlie died I got news of a rumour that was circulating around the village. The rumour was that I was out shopping when Charlie became ill. Rosie and Alice were supposed to have witnessed his dying moments alone, but the most disturbing image for me was that they had apparently been found, banging on the locked front door, screaming to get out, while their dead father lay in the next room. This ugly rumour left me profoundly upset at a time when I was little equipped to deal with any more emotional trauma. I never found out who thought up such a dramatic and inaccurate story, but I sincerely hope they felt ashamed when they discovered the truth.

Your children will probably receive many gifts and invitations to tea. People find the thought of a child who has just lost a mummy or daddy incredibly distressing, and they will want to do anything they can to help. Let people help you. Take up every offer because it will give you a chance to get a bit of peace, and the children will find the attentions of others very welcome when you are too distracted to give them much of yours. Your time will be taken up with the myriad of practical details that need to be addressed.

3

the funeral

finding an undertaker

When dealing with the practicalities of your partner's death, the first people you are likely to come into contact with are the funeral directors. Now, funeral directors are human, just like you and me, but none of us ever wants actually to have to deal with one – not unless they happen to look like Nate from *Six Feet Under*, in which case the funeral would frankly be a lot easier to bear. Undertakers do a great public service and it is often a thankless task, but we would prefer it if they just got on with it and left us alone. Sadly, we have to face the fact that we are going to have to form a close and often very emotional bond with them for a short while, and then hand over an obscene amount of money in order to make them go away.

I was exceedingly lucky when it came to my choice of under-taker – I was told by my GP that I had to get hold of one pretty quickly on the night of Charlie's death. The doctor gave me a choice of two: his first suggestion was the Co-op, and choosing them was quite out of the question because I knew Charlie would have tried to unzip his body bag rather than let the Co-op cart him away in a trail of little blue stamps. The other choice of undertaker was a man I had met at dinner on a number of occasions – but I never for a moment expected that I'd need to call on his professional services.

Tim Perring was charming and funny, totally different from the sombre, humourless image most of us have of funeral directors. He conducted all the formalities, from taking Charlie's body away to organising the funeral, with the utmost professionalism and tact, and I gave him a huge hug when the funeral was over because I knew that it couldn't have been done better.

choosing the coffin

I wanted a completely plain coffin with wooden handles, and that is exactly what I got. If you want to bury your partner in a cardboard box, then it is your right to do so. Coffins cannot be reused after a body has been laid in them, so after a cremation they are discarded and after burial they rot into the earth. Therefore, spending a fortune on the very best money can buy is, in my opinion, a waste of money. It might be worth thinking about making a donation to your partner's favourite charity, and in that way it would at least benefit the living. And if you can't afford to make a charitable donation, then you might consider saving your money for a really nice headstone because that, after all, is the lasting memorial to your partner.

the funeral service

Consideration must also be given to the person who will conduct the funeral service. This may be the first time you get to meet the vicar/rabbi/priest – and you may not like him or her when you do. When he or she comes to call, you might feel a huge sense of relief or, as in my case, you might get a sudden urge to embrace Satan and all his horrible, hairy incubi.

My vicar was not blessed with the gift of interpersonal skills. A scientist by choice and a vicar by calling, he really should have stuck with the Bunsen burner and the magnesium ribbon and left the sacraments well alone. He didn't say a prayer for my dead husband when he came to offer his condolences for the first time, nor, on a later occasion, did he comment on the order of service, despite knowing that Charlie's brother and I had laboured over it for the best part of a week. What he chose to give me in the way of comforting words was a statement on the poor state of Britain's road transport system. And do you know what? It didn't help at all – and I had really hoped that it would. After all, when you are worrying about contraflow systems, you completely forget that your husband has just died.

I was angry at his gawky embarrassment and total inability to confront my grief and I wanted him out of my house – but he wouldn't go. He wanted to carry on talking about roads, and even tried to enliven his chosen topic by including rail travel. Eventually Tim, the lovely undertaker, lured him away with the promise of a discussion on quantum physics and its effect on the Church, and peace returned to my house once more.

Tracy Jones had a similar experience when her husband, Clive, died:

We're not churchgoers but we wanted a church service. The vicar came to the house to talk to Clive's brothers, Clive's mum and me about the service, but it was awful because he just didn't talk! At all! We chaired the meeting, told him what hymns we wanted, who we wanted to speak and who would bear the coffin, because he didn't bother to ask those questions. He was completely mute; the only thing he did was nod. My family left me with him so that I could talk about Clive in private, and it was just the same. So much for the men of the cloth being good counsellors and knowing the words to give comfort; he said absolutely nothing. Throughout the meeting, in my dazed state, I literally thought it was a wind-up. I thought he was an imposter, and that we'd go to his car and find the real vicar tied up in the boot. It was surreal.

I'd written down reams of notes about Clive and our life together, which thankfully he took away with him. I was really worried about the service. On the day, three people from different aspects of Clive's life read personal tributes, which were brilliant and, thankfully, when the vicar spoke he virtually read out all I'd written, so it was a beautiful service in spite of him.

A wonderful vicar had married Charlie and me. He had since retired, but had been a good friend to us during our marriage, and he very kindly agreed to conduct the funeral service. It was vital to me that the vicar who spoke about Charlie, to a church packed with his closest friends, could do so with conviction and feeling. He did it beautifully, and I will be forever in his debt for the kindness he showed me at such a difficult time.

The service has to be right. I have a friend who thought she was in the wrong church when the vicar began to speak about her late husband. The vicar hadn't known the deceased man, but my friend had presumed that he would deliver a suitably moving tribute. And he did. It made her want to move right out of her seat and run screaming from the church because it bore absolutely no relation to the man she loved. She still talks about it with horror to this day.

Should the children be at the funeral?

You may be wondering whether or not to let your children attend the funeral. All I can say is if they ask to come, then let them. Babies will have no idea where they are, and toddlers will have little grasp of the importance of what you are doing; therefore it might be better if they were looked after elsewhere. Struggling with a tired toddler will only exacerbate your stress on an already stressful day, and will make the funeral even more difficult to cope with; so my advice is to err on the side of caution.

Older children really ought to have some say over whether or not they attend the funeral. Let them see their father or mother being buried; let them see the coffin in the crematorium; because if you allow your children to see what some might consider too upsetting for them, you stop them seeing their dead father on a bus, or their mother on a train, or riding in the back of a taxi.

For older children, not attending the funeral will result in a continuation of the disbelief about the death of their parent. My husband was seven years old when he lost his father, and never got over the trauma of not being allowed to attend his funeral. I was determined that Rosie would not go through life as he did, believing that daddy hadn't really died, but was a secret agent on a very special mission.

Robin Walker, who lost his wife, Zoe, to cancer on 11 September 2001, wrote this:

> For me the aftermath of September 11th helped, as the whole world seemed to be in a state of shock and it seemed appropriate that life was not normal (it must be hard to see the world carrying on as normal when your own has been inverted).
>
> I was unsure about taking my son Alex to the funeral, and had mixed reactions from family and friends (most of whom were probably too upset to contemplate the question). I found

discussing this with somebody at the children's bereavement charity 'Winston's Wish' useful. I thought Alex was too young to understand what the funeral was about and that he would probably not remember it in later years. The person I chatted to made me confront some issues such as how Alex will feel when he's older if he knows he wasn't there, but ultimately seemed to support my choice.

Many of our friends were great, as were my own parents who have become a great source of practical help (the best type of help in my experience). I spoke to some other bereaved fathers and found it useful to hear of their experience. Two of these found their Christian faith had helped them, but this wasn't something that would work for me. More usefully, I met up with another dad who had lost his wife to breast cancer a few years ago and who had a child just a little older than Alex. In the years that had passed he'd remarried, and hearing about how he had rebuilt his life and helped preserve his wife's memory for his daughter (they had a tree planted and visited it regularly), helped me a lot.

I knew what Charlie wanted me to do with his body after he died, because he had often mentioned how he loved the view from our village burial ground. He would never have openly spoken of his death to me, so without actually spelling it out, he told me exactly what I needed to know.

Most people would rather not discuss the method by which their body is disposed. It's not exactly the sort of conversation that any couple is likely to engage in, unless they absolutely have to. Therefore, in the absence of any clear instructions, you may be required to choose an appropriate method of interment for your partner. The decision is ultimately yours, but some consideration should be given to the wishes of any children who are old enough to voice an opinion, and also of other members of your partner's family. If you think your partner would have wished to be cremated and have his or her ashes scattered over some special place, then you should do what you think is best. The absence of a burial stone or memorial plaque may cause certain people to feel they have no place to visit when they wish to remember your partner, and this could potentially be a cause of friction, but I think that as long as you know you are acting in the best interests of your late partner, then you have to do as you see fit.

That's not to say that traditional burial sites don't also cause friction, as my friend Sarah found out to her cost. She discovered that another body had been buried far too close to her husband's grave, and then entered into a protracted row with the officious woman who was supposed to oversee the correct spacing of grave sites. Sarah found the whole affair extremely distressing and eventually had to have her late husband's remains dug up and moved to a different site. This row caused a lot of unnecessary distress nearly two years after the original burial, and the whole family was badly affected.

In the final event, all that matters is that you feel happy with your partner's final resting place, whether it is under a flowering cherry tree, or in an urn in the glove box of your car. In life you were connected and in death you should feel connected too.

What you choose to do is up to you entirely, but remember: what happens on the day of the funeral has the power to induce peace of mind or torment for a very long time afterwards.

commissioning a memorial

Once your partner has been buried or cremated, there is the question of how he or she should be remembered. The choice of memorial stone is one of the most important decisions you will have to make, but it is not one that should be rushed. If your partner has been buried, it will take at least six months before the ground has settled enough to allow a headstone to be fitted. In that time you can visit graveyards and get some idea of what you want. But it may not be until sometime later that you can actually bring yourself to think about commissioning a memorial.

If you take a walk around most modern graveyards, you will notice that, by and large, the headstones are remarkably similar – they are either shiny, black marble with gold lettering, white marble with black lettering, or rough-hewn granite with a smooth face and carved or raised lettering. When you are ready to buy a memorial, the choice of stone and style is entirely up to you, but let me add a note of caution about rushing into a decision. If you take a walk around any Norman churchyard, you will see headstones dating right back to 1700 and earlier. What is apparent about these ancient stones is that, by and large, the lettering is still legible. Letters that have been cut into stone will, depending on the hardness of the stone, remain readable for hundreds of years. The Victorians brought memorial masonry to a high art, and the extraordinary craftsmanship of the stonemasons of the time can be seen by walking around a Victorian graveyard. These crafts still exist; artistry still exists; but for the majority of the population, the choice of memorial has to be made from an exceedingly limited selection of headstones, which lack any notion of originality or art.

The problem with the majority of headstones these days is that the lettering used to mark the last resting place of your beloved is going to fade or fall off after a relatively short amount of time; and while gilding may look nice when it is new, it doesn't last. The simplest and most effective headstone is plain stone, with machine or hand-cut lettering. There are many memorial masons and specialist stonecutters who can be commissioned to produce a unique headstone, which will outlast all of the mass-produced memorials around it.

There is a charity called 'Memorials By Artists', run by Harriet Frazer, which was set up to help people commission memorials of any type. It is possible, for instance, to commission an object in silver, a single ceramic tile, a wooden or stone seat, a sundial, a single pane or window of engraved or stained glass, a sculpture, a fountain or a folly. Some of these items will be expensive, but if you just need inspiration then visit the website www.memorialsbyartists.co.uk and you might get some ideas.

I didn't know what to do about Charlie's headstone, but once I had discovered that all memorials didn't have to look the same, I decided to set about finding a stonemason to produce some-thing that would reflect the unique man Charlie had been. I happened to be walking in our village square one day and noticed a stonemason's van outside the church. I went into the church and spoke to the stonemason; he did look rather surprised when I said I wanted to commission a headstone for my husband (maybe he thought we'd just had a really big row and I was trying to let off a bit of steam), but eventually we were able to have a fruitful discussion on the subject of death. I had gained some inspiration regarding the style of lettering I wanted from reading the 'Memorials By Artists' booklet, and once I had shown him a sample, he set about drawing a scale copy of the inscription I had chosen for the headstone.

There is no need to think that a personalised memorial is going to be prohibitively expensive. I paid just over £1,000 for Charlie's headstone in 1998, but for that I got a magnificently crafted piece of plain Cornish slate, with soft, chamfered edges and beautifully sharp, hand-cut lettering in the Arts and Crafts style, which will last for a couple of hundred years at least. The stone is a work of art, and when I sent a large tip to the stone-mason for doing such a fantastic job, he sent it back to me and told me to spend the money on my children instead.

Sometimes death gives us gifts, and meeting Mr Piper, a true craftsman and a gentleman, was one of those gifts.

The epitaph

The most difficult decision I faced was the choice of epitaph. I wanted it to explain why Charlie had died so young, but also to make people understand what a brave man he'd been. I spent many nights thinking about the exact wording, and then it came to me:

> *They Said His Heart Was Weak*
> *No Heart Was Ever Stronger*

You should never rush into choosing an epitaph. It is vitally important that what you choose to put on the headstone is both personal and pertinent to the person buried beneath it. There is no hurry; once your partner has been buried or cremated you have as long as you want to find the right words.

> If you have children then it might be a good idea to involve them in designing the headstone. A simple sketch or inscription could be engraved on the back of the headstone, and in that way your children would feel that they have played an important part in the commissioning of the memorial.

Having somewhere to go and reflect on the loss of a parent is vitally important to any child, and if that child knows there is a personal addition to the headstone, he or she will feel much more connected to the burial place and better disposed to visit. Children need a sense of place, but graveyards can be grim and sombre places; there are too many angels of death and not enough sunflowers. The future lies with our children, so we should do everything we can to help them to accept their loss.

In summary

Here are a few points it might be wise to consider when organising the funeral:

■ Don't be pressured into spending a fortune on funeral expenses.

■ Make sure the vicar/priest/rabbi is sympathetic to your needs, and is willing to conduct the funeral service according to your wishes.

■ Give careful consideration to the needs of your children when deciding whether to let them attend the funeral, and be aware of the impact non-attendance might have on their ability to come to terms with their grief.

■ Don't feel guilty if you don't feel like crying at the funeral – it will be a surreal day and there will be plenty of time for tears in the months that follow.

■ Don't rush into choosing a headstone or memorial. It takes at least six months for the ground to settle at a burial site, and you can use this time to look at other headstones and think about a suitable epitaph.

■ Don't feel you have to opt for a headstone from the Co-op window. You have the right to choose exactly what you want, and there are hundreds of skilled stonemasons and letter-carvers who would be happy to provide a unique and lasting memorial to your loved one.

■ There may be restrictions governing the style of headstone that you are able to choose, so it would be wise to check with the relevant authorities before you proceed.

4

practicalities

Funerals are expensive things. So are solicitors, gravestones, burial plots, cremation vases and wreaths. Money will be haemorrhaging out of your bank account and you will be too distracted to keep an eye on where it is going. Many people leave all the financial aspects of the relationship to their partner, so it comes as a great shock to them when they have to sit down and go through all of the household bills and financial affairs.

It pays to be methodical. If you cannot think straight, then find someone you trust to sit with you while you sort through all the documents that need to be looked at. But be warned – if your partner was a secretive person, you may find something you didn't bargain for.

secrets and lies

I have a friend who had to go through his father's chest of drawers in the garage because he didn't want his mother to discover the stash of porn that was hidden there. Even though he knew of the magazines' existence, he was a little surprised at their content – in particular, one volume rather charmingly titled *Knotty*, which on closer inspection detailed various couples' fascination with being bound up with household string. I'm not suggesting for a moment that you will find anything quite so bizarre, but if you had any suspicions about your partner then it might be wise to brace yourself, just in case.

But sometimes secrets and lies cannot be forgotten or forgiven so easily. Finding out unexpected revelations about a person you thought you knew intimately can be utterly devastating. One widow, who wishes to remain anonymous, wrote this:

My husband collapsed from a heart attack in front of me while we were attending a function with a number of friends. He died shortly afterwards, having never regained consciousness. The shock was terrific as he was in his mid-50s and, as far as I knew, quite fit.

However, a couple of days later things came to light and I began to unravel a horror story. Luckily my two daughters and son-in-law were with me when I discovered about his long-term mistress. And it took a month to discover the full extent of the huge amount of debts that he had built up.

To go from being a stunned, bereaved widow to an angry and betrayed widow, with no hope of getting answers from the man you thought you knew, is something I wouldn't be able to explain to anyone who hasn't gone through it. I discovered many, many ways in which he had lied to me, and now it's hard to remember any of the last 17 years with any certainty of what was true about them where he is concerned.

I found that my anger was able to keep me going but that the love and help of friends and family was the ultimate strength that I drew on. One thing I did that helped me quite a lot is that early on, I sat down and typed and typed and typed when the hurt was at its worst. I put down what had happened and felt that I almost screamed into the PC as I tried to express my feelings. It's definitely something that helped me and I haven't added any more to it for a long time.

money matters

The main feeling that will pervade your confused mental state at this time is one of panic; panic about money. You will be wondering how you can pay for everything: the mortgage, household bills and loans. If you were not employed at the time of your partner's death, then you are going to have to think about getting a job, and if you have children you will need someone to take care of them while you are at work. All these things need addressing; figures and bills will swim before your eyes but you will be too out of it to make any sense of them. What you need more than anything at this time is sensible financial advice, and there are many ways of getting it before you have to resort to paying for the services of a financial advisor. If you are lucky, and if they are able, your parents will be desperate to help you in any way they can – so let them. If they offer to give you a loan to help tide you over, then take it, even if that means you have to endure your mother's cooking every Sunday. And if all your parents offer is advice, then you should listen to them – unless they are both compulsive gamblers, in which case I think it might be best to ignore them.

This is the time when you are at your most vulnerable. You will feel like kissing the feet of anyone who offers to give you anything, and if they are twisted enough to have an ulterior motive then you will not see it coming.

You wouldn't see it coming even if it telephoned you beforehand to tell you it was on the way, and then arrived wearing a T-shirt saying, 'I'm an ulterior motive and I'm going to take advantage of you.' So I would strongly urge you to seek help at the Citizens Advice Bureau. They employ experts in a variety of different fields, and you will be amazed at what they will be able to help you with.

running the home

If you were the main breadwinner and have been left with children to support, then the major worry will not be on how you manage financially, but on how you take care of your children and the house, and hold down your job at the same time. For a widower, the whole emphasis of grief is different from that of a widow. In losing your partner, you have lost the nurturing side of the partnership. Your partner provided the softness, the understanding and the mothering side of the relationship. She may have done most of the cooking and cleaning, and will almost certainly have had the most input in bringing up your children. If this was not the case, then you should have some idea of how to manage your household affairs and take care of the children, but what is much more likely is that you will now be feeling lost, vulnerable, and desperately in need of help. It is vitally important that you don't rush into anything at this point. Take some time off work and try to establish a list of priorities for yourself and your children.

One man wrote and told me about the shock of having to get his three children ready for school the day after his wife died. He had absolutely no idea what to give his children for their packed lunch, having always left that side of things to his wife. When you are struggling to hold your family and yourself together, it is the seemingly straightforward jobs that suddenly become Herculean tasks. I'm sure many men find themselves in a similar position when they lose their wife, but there is no easy solution to the problem of taking care of all those mundane household tasks.

Richard Martin, a 52-year-old widower, wrote this:

Basic things around the house suddenly became a big issue. Learning to use the washing machine, ironing a shirt and cooking were quite a challenge initially. I was saved by the fact that my daughter had temporarily returned to live at home a few weeks before Sally's death and is currently still here. In the meantime I have become reasonably competent at all these things, but for many widowers this does add to the difficulties of coping alone.

It is important not to let yourself get bogged down with unnecessary jobs at this time. The housework can wait, but you really ought to think about writing a list of priorities so that you are clear about what needs to be done immediately and what can be put off for a week or so. If you have children, then they have to come first. You should try to ensure that they have clean clothes and a freshly laundered school uniform at the beginning of each week. They should be encouraged to help out around the house as much as possible, but here I must sound a note of caution. If you are a widower with daughters over about eight years of age, then it is vitally important that you don't place a burden of responsibility on your oldest daughter. She will already be feeling the need to help around the house as much as possible, but if she is made to feel that it is her role to become a surrogate mother to the rest of the family, then you might be storing up a whole lot of trouble and associated guilt, which could potentially be very harmful as she reaches adolescence. Exactly the same rule applies to an eldest son who has lost his father. If he offers to help out, that is wonderful, but if you make him feel that it is his duty to take over his father's role in the home, then he might end up becoming a very bitter and resentful young man. If your children feel they are being expected to behave like adults, they might also feel that they should handle their emotions in an adult way, and that could be terrifically damaging to them in the long run. Let your children feel that they are helping you without making them feel it is their duty to do so. It will probably take many weeks before you establish any kind of domestic order, but your children will understand.

Wash-day blues

Housework is something you will have to face sooner or later, and it has to be said that two of the most soul-destroying words in the English language are 'washing' and 'ironing'. Granted, they will seem relatively inoffensive to a person who is struggling with 'death' and 'grief', but they are depressing all the same. There are three ways of dealing with your laundry:

1. Don't do it. Wear the same clothes every day and beat them into a corner with a big stick each night.
2. Wear only Crimplene and nylon – you may become a fire risk, but at least your clothes will drip-dry and never need ironing.
3. Bite the bullet and tackle your smalls.

The first solution isn't a solution, it's a cop-out. If you don't want to become even more of a social pariah than you already are, it is essential that you remain moderately presentable. Quentin Crisp once said that he possessed only two pairs of underwear, and that he rarely bothered to wash them because the spare pair would always be slightly less offensive than the ones he was wearing. You could try to adopt his rather novel approach to laundry, but sooner or later you are going to have to become acquainted with the washing machine. Wearing only man-made fibres is certainly one solution – BBC engineers have been doing it for years and it doesn't seem to have adversely affected their reputation as lady-killers and fashion icons . . . which leaves the final option.

There are few more depressing sights than a basket full of un-ironed clothes. You may never have used an iron before, and if you went from the comfort of having a mother who did your laundry straight to a partner who took care of your washing and made sure you had a crisp, clean shirt for work each morning, then you may be in for a bit of a shock. Doing the washing can be a very complicated business and is often fraught with danger: white becomes grey, elastic sags, bobbles appear and socks vanish. But don't be put off; washing is really easy if you remember a few simple rules:

1. Keep dark and light clothes separate.
2. Read the washing instructions on labels. Don't wash anything except cotton at more than 60 degrees – unless you like tight sweaters.
3. Watch out for stray purple pants that may be lurking in your white pile. They are not only wrong in every sense of the word, they also have the ability to wreak havoc with the rest of your wash, so it pays to be vigilant. If you do have a catastrophe, there are many products on the market that will

rectify any mishaps. Such products will make your grey whites white again, and will reverse any purple colour runs. But don't expect miracles.

4. Try to be disciplined about doing your washing – there is nothing more repellent than the smell of stale sweat; and trying to disguise the smell with a liberal dousing of Old Spice will only add to the problem. We all love the scent of a man, but not a dirty, malodorous man.

5. Accept the fact that there will always be at least one odd sock at the end of each wash. It's one of life's little mysteries.

Ironing

Once you have successfully completed your washing duties, the next big hurdle is ironing. Nobody likes to iron; some people tolerate it and others positively detest it. But the simple fact is that unless you have a big, bad American tumble dryer or an accommodating cleaning lady, there are some things you will have to tackle by hand. If you try to stick to what you know and take the easy way out by investing in a Corby trouser press, you will soon come unstuck. That particular labour-saving device may make light work of a pair of Farrah slacks after a night in a Travelodge, but trying to stuff a crumpled king-size duvet cover into its welcoming jaws may prove to be a little more difficult.

Ironing is all about heat and steam, and if you have enough of both, then you will be able to get through just about anything. Silk should be treated with care, as should children's T-shirts with pictures on the front. The pictures are often plasticised and I know from experience just how much damage they can do to a new iron (turning clothes inside out will prevent any disasters). You don't have to iron your duvet covers or your sheets. Folding them carefully when damp and putting them into a warm airing cupboard will make them reasonably presentable. And anyway, if you are not interested in eating and you can't sleep, then you are hardly going to notice a few wrinkles in your bed linen.

The clothes you wear are a little more important. It may seem reasonable to go out in a crumpled pair of trousers and a dirty, creased shirt, or a pair of leggings and a baggy sweater; it's much less effort for you and I'm sure people will understand why you aren't quite as well presented as usual. But I believe that wearing clean, well-ironed clothes makes us feel better about ourselves.

> If you look a mess then you will invariably feel the same, and even if you feel you have nothing to look forward to each morning, then at least the sight of clean socks, pants and a freshly laundered shirt may make getting out of bed a little easier for you.

Ironing is really only difficult if you make it so. You can get a lot of thinking done when you are ironing; you can also watch television or listen to the radio. Once you have established a routine for doing it, then it should cease to be such a daunting and depressing prospect.

Cooking

Cooking for the family for the first time might come as a hell of a shock to the system. If you want to feed the children on pop tarts and Sugar Puffs in the first few days after your partner's death then go right ahead – they will understand, and social services won't be called in unless you do something really gross like making your children eat broad beans and broccoli every day. If you are really lucky, then your friends will step in and give you a hand. Robin Walker had the following experience:

I have some vivid memories of how awful things were at this time, and clearly remember the undertaker saying my wife's name while handing me a plastic bag containing her ashes in a jar. Going to the supermarket for the first time was unexpectedly difficult as there are a lot of simple choices you normally make that you may have to change. I remember putting a jar of Marmite back on the shelf (only Zoe liked it) and feeling how awful it all was.

For more about cooking, see pages 71–78.

childcare

If you have young children and have to return to work, then finding suitable childcare will become your main priority. This is a minefield – I would be lying if I said otherwise – and throwing money at the problem is not the solution. The only way to make sure you are employing somebody who will care for your children as you would want them to be cared for is to trust your gut instinct.

First, if you employed anybody to look after the children before your partner died, and they were good at their job, then find out if they can work for you on a full-time basis. It is vitally important that you can establish trust and familiarity, and if the children already know their nanny, then you lessen the chances of them being upset and confused. If you have to start from scratch, it is important to think about the implications of your choice of carer. If you decide on an au pair, because he or she will be able to cook and clean as well as taking care of the children, then try to choose one who speaks fluent English. The problems your children are likely to encounter cannot be dealt with by grunting and nodding; it's no good getting a blonde bombshell from Latvia who has looks to die for, but who can't tell when your child is upset or provide any sympathy other than an occasional Slavic shrug. The other problem with au pairs is that they tend to be transitory. If your children become attached to their au pair, just imagine how they will feel when he or she has to leave. You can do your children irreparable damage if they are presented with a succession of temporary 'mothers' who only last six months before a replacement appears on the scene. Think about the children, and only the children, at this time.

Robin Walker told me about his experiences of childcare:

The main thing that helped me cope over the first few months was having a full-time nanny to help me look after Alex, even though this was expensive. Unless you have close family or friends who can offer continuous childcare then I'd say get external help. It can be hard to look after young children at the best of times but when you have just lost your partner it can be close to impossible. Alex, like most young children, responds to new, difficult, frustrating and frightening experiences by changes in his behaviour (not improvements of course). His sleep pattern was disturbed and he'd wake up throughout the night, and as I was having problems sleeping the overall effect was to leave me feeling exhausted and unable to cope at times. My employers (University of London) were great and gave me a term off on compassionate leave, and I do not think I could have coped with my grief and job at that time.

Nannies

Nanny agencies are often expensive and sometimes totally ineffectual – often all you get for your money is a single contact number. Most of them will promise that the girls have been fully vetted, but I would advise caution. If you are a widower having to interview female applicants, then it would be advisable to get a female friend over who has children of her own – that way you will have a second opinion and it will also be more seemly to have another female present. If my experience with nannies is anything to go by, it doesn't matter how many qualifications they have; all that matters is that they get on with your children and they get on with you. I would go for experience over qualifications every time. If you can find an older woman who has had her own children, then at least you know she will be able to change a nappy, and that she won't panic if something goes wrong.

I have a friend who took on a young nanny from a respected local agency. On her first day the girl was left with instructions on how to heat up supper for her young charge. The instructions were 'three minutes in the microwave', but somehow, over the course of a hectic day, those instructions turned into '30 minutes in the microwave'. Now, you would think that common sense would dictate that 30 minutes is a mite too long to reheat fish pie, but the young girl was unfamiliar with the workings of a microwave and went ahead with the cremation of the boy's supper, quite oblivious to the smell of burning and strange noises that were coming from the infernal device.

When my friend came home and enquired about her son's supper, the nanny told her what she'd done and said that the boy had been able to eat a few of the peas that 'weren't too black'. She hadn't thought to throw the whole lot away and give him a ham sandwich instead. She had her instructions and she would not deviate from them, no matter what. Needless to say that was her first and last day at work.

When Charlie died I had to go back to work, but having had a very bad experience with an agency nanny I decided to try my luck with an advert in the local newspaper. I interviewed three women: the first seemed quite nice, but then a friend phoned to tell me she had been sacked from her last job for stealing. The second woman would not have looked out of place selling lucky heather; she wore a large sovereign ring on each of her chunky fingers and had more earrings than was absolutely necessary. Her interest was not in the children (she didn't even ask their names) but in how much she would be earning. I had visions of returning home to find one of my girls bearing the imprint of George V on her rosy cheek, and so I didn't call her back. The next candidate seemed perfect; she was an older woman who had brought up two children of her own. She asked me over to see her house, so that I could see for myself that she was a clean and tidy person. I took the children over to see her and she told me that the house was tidy because her carer had just been to visit. Apparently, she had a carer to help her cope with the effects of chronic ME, but didn't see that it would be a hindrance to her when it came to looking after my children – apart from the fact that she would need a nap every afternoon. I was getting a little uncomfortable about the thought of her napping while my young daughters were left to their own devices, but decided to give her the benefit of the doubt. When she told me that her husband used to beat her up and that she had been abused as a child, I decided that I had heard enough. She had been very honest, but I couldn't take on that level of emotional baggage when I was struggling to carry my own.

I had just about given up hope when I got a call from a Geordie angel. She had a grown-up child of her own but no qualifications to speak of. As soon as I spoke to her I knew she was right for the job. Being a mother in her own right gave her all the skills she needed to look after my two little girls; she came into our lives and has never left. I consider myself extremely lucky to have found such a wonderful nanny. It was pure chance that I found her, but sometimes you need a bit of luck – and she was mine.

Childcare tips

1. Finding good childcare is a minefield – so trust your instincts.
2. Nannies can be prohibitively expensive, so it may be better to send a young child to a day nursery. For older children, an after-school club is a great option, and will help to stop your child feeling isolated.
3. If you do opt for a nanny or an au pair, pay careful attention to how he or she interacts with your children on first meeting them.
4. Don't rush into anything.
5. Don't hire anybody who can't speak English fluently.
6. Don't rely solely on the recommendation of an agency – a personal recommendation is what you need.
7. If you are a widower, get a female friend who has children to help you vet any prospective candidates.
8. Don't expect your children to give their new nanny/au pair an easy ride, or be able to slot straight into a day-nursery without any problems – they will be extremely vulnerable and needy, and you are the one who must provide comfort and reassurance.

5

a helping hand

If I had one piece of good advice to offer the recently bereaved, it would be this: when somebody comes up to you and says, 'Just let me know if there is anything I can do – anything at all', say to them, 'It's not now that I need you; please come back in six months and ask me then.'

At first you are too numb to ask for help, so you nod weakly and say, 'Thank you, I'll let you know.' But what you should really do is present the person who is offering to help you with a carefully compiled list, which he or she would then be required to study before making a selection. This would be most effectively done at the funeral, where you have lots of people who cannot rush away. The list would contain all the useful things that would help you out in the months to come. For widows it would include such essentials as looking after the children, mowing the lawn, mending the washing machine, chopping wood, unscrewing jars, invitations to supper, listening and hugging – lots of hugging. For widowers it would include looking after the children, doing the shopping, hand relief, sewing on buttons, hand relief, ironing, washing, changing nappies, cooking, cleaning and hand relief. The friend in question would be required to honour his or her promise, at a time specified by you, and everybody would be happy.

Or not.

a friend in need

Obligation is a serious thing. People feel obliged to say they will help you, but often have no real intention of honouring that obligation. People offer to help, half hoping that you will never take up their offer. It is a wonderful thing indeed to have so many people wishing to help you, but come the time when you have to call in the favour, you will discover a little more about human frailty than you really wanted to know. It is one of the gifts you are to be blessed with; you won't really see it as a gift at the time, but eventually your insight into the human psyche will prove a valuable asset.

It seems that since the death of Princess Diana, we, as a nation, have become rather fascinated with public displays of grief. People now appear to be compelled to bring flowers and gifts to murder scenes and child abduction sites, and it seems that wherever there are cameras, there are now teddy bears and remembrance bouquets, sad-faced men and weeping women. Why do people behave in such a way?

Princess Diana's death turned public grieving into a new pastime. Florists have never had it so good; in fact, I'm surprised there isn't a new magazine called *Goodbye!*, devoted to capturing shots of celebrity mourners and quirky floral displays. What do those people, those people who drive 20 miles to drop off a cuddly teddy bear or a bunch of daffodils, really feel? Do they feel deep sorrow for the dead? Or do they feel like they should be seen to be feeling deep sorrow, and that if they are filmed placing a tribute at a murder site they will be somehow elevated in the eyes of their peers? Do those same people offer an equal amount of sympathy to people who are not in the public eye? Would the man with the sad face bother to drive 20 miles to drop off a meal to a friend who had lost a wife? I hope he would, but something tells me that helping a friend or colleague to get through bereavement takes a whole lot more effort and commitment than throwing a few flowers at a passing hearse.

I would hate anybody to think that I did not appreciate every single act of kindness that was shown to me in the first weeks of my widowhood – I did and I still do. The point I am trying to make is that while it is very heartening to receive offers of help, what you need more than anything else is not an offer but a deed.

> Finding a casserole on your doorstep will mean more to you than any amount of sympathetic words. Being asked out to lunch with your children will make you feel more loved than a hundred offers of help. And why is that? Because you didn't have to ask.

I have friends in my village who cooked for me when they knew I didn't have the heart to cook for myself. Six years later they still come over every so often, bringing with them something delicious on a tray. They love me and don't expect anything in return, they do it because they loved my husband and just want to make me happy now that he is gone. That sums up the true nature of friendship to me, and if you are lucky enough to have friends like mine, then I know you will find the first few weeks a whole lot easier to cope with.

Of course you cannot make people help you in practical ways. If all you ever get are offers of help, then you might have to pluck up the courage to ask. If somebody offers to look after your children, then drop a note through their door asking them to have them on a certain day – that will give them time to think about it and means you don't have to ask them face to face. If they really meant their offer then they will make every effort to accommodate your wishes. If they say they cannot help you on that particular day but offer help on another day, then you know that they do genuinely want to help. If, however, they find an excuse and never offer to help you again, you know they were not sincere in the first place.

> Don't feel proud. Take up every offer of help, however small, because there will soon come a time when the offers dry up and you are left to cope on your own.

family support

Families are supposed to come to your aid in times of crisis, and for most of us that is exactly what happens. But in some cases, our immediate family members – or those of our partner – can react in a totally inappropriate way that causes untold hurt and distress at an already stressful time.

One woman wrote to me on this subject and I wanted to use her e-mail as an example of how relatives can react to death:

My husband, who was five years my junior, dropped dead at my best friend's 40th birthday party which we had organised. He had never complained, never been ill, never even had the common cold for the last four years. He was my lover, best friend, dancing partner and personal comedian! We had been together for 12 years and I have two children, one aged 17 (previous marriage) and our daughter who is now 10.

The reason for this e-mail is his parents – we never got on fantastically when my husband was alive but had never fallen out. I always felt that they never quite liked me – but hey – it never affected my relationship with my husband. We would have them for dinner etc. and I was always respectful.

After the death of my husband, my father-in-law turned into what I can only describe as a complete raving lunatic who saw me as the murderer of my husband. I involved my in-laws in every aspect of my husband's burial and saw them as much as I could for their support. I am very lucky and have loving parents and two brothers and two sisters.

When the abuse from my father-in-law started, I understood his anger and actually went along with the concept of 'Oh well – if he is going to take it out on someone it might as well be me.'

This lasted for six to eight weeks. By the eighth week I could take no more and the worm turned – I am now in a situation where he does not see his granddaughter – she does not want to see him and he has made no attempt to see her.

I also heard from a woman who was conned out of a large sum of money and then persuaded to move house by relatives who now cross the road to avoid her. All of this happens at a time of confusion and weakness. Death prompts people to react in strange and unexpected ways, and many of their unusual and unwanted attentions will be directed at you. Because you are dealing with family members, you may not be able to be as forthright as you would under normal circumstances, so it is vitally important that you have a friend outside the family upon whom you can rely to get a second opinion.

You must remember that there are people around you who are also experiencing grief, and you cannot be sure how that grief will manifest itself. If you are lucky, then your family, and that of your partner, will be immensely supportive, and will recognise that you need time and space to come to terms with your loss. But if there are any flaws within your relationship, you can be sure that small cracks will become gaping chasms under the intense pressure that death places upon us all.

My advice is to think only of yourself at this time. It may seem like a selfish concept, but you cannot afford to devote your precious emotional resources to people who do not have your best interests at heart.

> Death brings out the best and the worst in people, and you will see and hear all sorts of terrible things over the course of your first few weeks as a widow or widower.

If you bend under pressure from family members at this time then you might never recover, so if you feel that others are being unreasonable and you cannot face an argument, then you have to distance yourself until you are better equipped to address the problem. Don't feel that you have to see people who are causing you pain just because they were related to your partner or are related to you. You will know in your heart what is right. Even through the fog of grief you will be able to tell the difference between kindness and interference, but the ability to act upon your instincts will not be regained for some time to come. Therefore, the easiest way for you to deal with potentially harmful problems is to isolate yourself from them. Try not to do or say anything that might add to your troubles, unless a situation is becoming unbearable.

I heard from a man recently whose mother-in-law took it upon herself to come to the house and sort out all of his late wife's clothes only days after her death. The woman had decided what her son-in-law would want, without even bothering to consult him, and he was too shocked to argue. When she mentioned that she was going to post all of the Christmas presents that her late daughter had left on top of the wardrobe, the man decided to act. He asked a colleague at work what he should do and she recommended that he read my site. The next day he told his mother-in-law to leave his wife's clothes where they were and asked her not to interfere in his affairs unless asked to do so.

It's not just women who feel defenceless in the face of grief – men feel just the same way, and sometimes a mother-in-law is the scariest thing on God's earth. If you stand up for what you believe is right and then end up having a big row, then so what? Nobody died, did they?

In summary

- Expect people to make promises they do not keep.
- Having inside information about a sudden death gets you noticed, and many of your so-called friends might use your suffering as a way to get attention. You may think they are your friends, but as soon as the initial excitement has died down you won't see them for dust.
- Make sure you have a few good friends around you whom you can trust implicitly and rely on for long-term support.
- Death can make people act very strangely. If this affects you adversely then you have to accept that the people who are making you unhappy are expendable. Think only of your own happiness at this time, know your friends and recognise that in times of intense stress good people come forward and worthless people retreat into the shadows.
- Relatives can be a nightmare. Don't feel obliged to be nice to them if they are making your life hell.
- Don't let yourself be bullied into making rash decisions by relatives, just because you feel a family obligation.
- Don't be surprised if your late partner's family become resentful or even openly hostile. They too are feeling loss and may use you as the focus of their grief.
- Try not to be too hard on people at this time. Friends who have not experienced death cannot begin to comprehend how you are feeling, and those who have lost a parent or a friend may tell you that they know how you are feeling – they don't, but if they offer you help, then take it.

6

facing the world

When I went to collect Charlie's death certificate, in an ideal world I would have been given a minder, bearing a wad of leaflets. The minder would have been employed to walk in front of me when I appeared in public, distributing the leaflets to anyone who looked likely to approach me.

On the leaflets would be the following statement:

Her husband has just died.

No, she didn't expect it.

This was as much a shock for her as it is for you.

If you feel too paralysed with embarrassment to talk to her about it, then please pretend you haven't seen her; walk past and think about what you would like to say to her when you next meet.

If you do want to speak to her then please think very carefully about what you want to say. I would suggest asking how she is, listening for a minute or so, and then saying goodbye.

It's not that she doesn't want to talk to you; it's just that she can't. She can't talk to anybody at the moment without breaking down.

Thank you for your co-operation.

Of course it would have been impractical, but it would have saved an awful lot of distress.

Once the funeral is over you will feel like retreating from the world because being invisible is better than having to get out and face people. It is sad but true that some of the most painful words you are likely to hear will come from well-meaning people who feel that saying something totally inappropriate is better than saying nothing at all. Glib statements are painful at the best of times, but in the first few days after your partner's death they will be unbearable. Ill-chosen words have the ability to penetrate the numbed-out world you inhabit like tiny darts of consciousness. They wake you up; they remind you of what you are and where you are. They hurt.

C.S. Lewis compared the feeling of having to appear in public soon after being widowed as a kind of leprosy. People will avoid you, not because they are afraid of coming away from a handshake with more fingers than they started with, but because they find it too difficult to know what to say. But sometimes it is impossible to avoid people; you cannot hide away forever, and when you do go out there will be nothing about your demeanour that suggests anything other than total normality. You will have to tell all sorts of people news that will shock them into silence. You will have to say it in shops, at school, on the bus and at work. You will have to make yourself say words that wound you with every syllable. You will have to repeat those words over and over again through your own tears and the wide-eyed disbelief of the person you are telling. And somewhere along the line there will be an unthinking person who listens to those words and then says, 'Sorry to hear about your wife, but you'll soon meet somebody else.' Or 'Time is a great healer.' Or 'So, how are you managing without a husband?' Or, 'Buy a kitten.' Or some other rubbish they have picked up in a supermarket self-help book and which they think qualifies them to tell you how you should be feeling right now. You can't escape them – all you can do is pity them, turn your back and walk away.

> People use platitudes as a replacement for personal experience, substituting insensitivity for insight.
> Platitude schmatitude.
> If in doubt, don't say it.

In summary

■ Accept that people will say terrible things to you.

■ No matter what people might say, buying a kitten will not make you forget your dead partner.

■ People speak clumsily but often have kind hearts. One act of kindness is worth a thousand words.

■ Ill-considered platitudes will wound you, but there is nothing you can do to shield yourself from the thoughtless words of others.

■ If you go out in public and don't want to be bothered, wear ear plugs, look down at the ground and walk fast. Alternatively, get a clipboard and pretend to be conducting a market research survey – that way nobody will stop and talk to you.

7

mourning conventions

The Victorians were uncompromising when it came to facing the world. They wore their grief; they wore death about them so that all the world could see they were suffering, and could react accordingly. The trouble with our society is that death and grief are supposed to be kept away from public view. Because we have no outward signs that we are grief-stricken, we are supposed to act as if nothing has happened; we are supposed to lock it all away to save the embarrassment of those around us, and to save them the trouble of having to recognise our pain and deal with its many manifestations.

> The Victorians were very up-front about death. Poverty and disease were rife, and even the wealthiest of people were not excluded from the unwelcome attentions of the Grim Reaper.

Victorian polite society was as tightly laced as a whalebone corset; even in death there were formalities to observe, and failure to do so was socially unacceptable. The death of Prince Albert made a widow of Queen Victoria. Her very public display of grief and the length of time that it affected her were seen by her subjects as a mark of how deeply she loved her husband. Her mourning also set the tone for how the rest of society should mourn.

widow's weeds

A Victorian widow was expected to withdraw totally from society, to display the weight of her sorrow for everyone to see, and to make herself both invisible and inaccessible to men. There was a very strict code of mourning dress – you couldn't just throw on any old dress that was vaguely dark and expect to be able to stroll in the park or visit the theatre. Any suggestion of gaiety would be frowned upon, and widows had to wear what they were told to wear, as we can see from this extract, taken from *Collier's Cyclopaedia*, published in 1901:

It will be as well to consider in succession the different degrees of mourning, and their duration. The widow's is the deepest mourning of all. The following list would be ample for a widow's outfit. We have given a rather large one because, of course, it can be curtailed as wished.

One best dress of Henrietta trimmed entirely with crepe.

One dress, either a costume of Cyprus crepe, or an old black dress trimmed with rainproof crepe.

One Henrietta mantle lined with silk and deeply trimmed with crepe.

One warmer jacket of cloth lined, trimmed with crepe.

One bonnet of best silk crepe, with long veil.

One bonnet of rainproof crepe, with crepe veil.

Twelve collars and cuffs of muslin or lawn, with deep hems. Several sets must be provided, say six of each kind.

One black stiff petticoat.

Four pair of black hose, either silk, cashmere, or spun silk.

Twelve handkerchiefs with black borders for ordinary use, cambric.

Twelve of finer cambric for better occasions.

Caps, either of lisse, tulle or tarlatan – shape depending very much on the age. Young widows wear chiefly the Marie Stuart shape, but all widows' caps have long streamers. If in summer a parasol should be required, it should be of silk deeply trimmed with crepe, almost covered with it, but no lace or fringe for the first year. Afterward mourning fringe may be put on. A muff, if required, would be made of dark fur or of Persian lamb.

The first mourning is worn for twelve months. Second mourning twelve months also; the cap in second mourning is left off, and the crepe no longer covers the dresses, but is put on in tucks. Elderly widows frequently remain in mourning for long periods, if not for the remainder of their lives, retaining the widow's cap, collar and cuffs, but leaving off the deep crepe the second year, and afterwards entirely discarding crepe, but wearing mourning materials such as Victoria cords, Janus cords, cashmere, and so on.

No ornaments are worn in such deep mourning, except jet, for the first year. Rich silk is, of course, admissible in widows' mourning, especially for evening wear, but it must always be deeply trimmed with crepe for the first year, and the quantity afterwards gradually lessened.

Widow's lingerie, to be always nice, entails a considerable amount of expense. If collars, cuffs and caps are made at home, as we before said, they get soiled directly.

Duration of mourning: Widow's first mourning lasts for a year and a day. Second mourning cap left off, less crepe and silk for nine months (some curtail it to six), remaining three months of second year plain black without crepe, and jet ornaments. At the end of the second year the mourning can be put off entirely; but it is better taste to wear half mourning for at least six months longer; and, as we have before mentioned, many widows never wear colours any more, unless for some solitary event, such as the wedding of a child, when they would probably put it off for the day.

No invitations would be accepted before the funeral of any relatives closely enough related to you to put on mourning for. In the case of brothers, sisters, parents and grandparents, society would be given up for at least three months, if not more, and it would be very bad taste to go to a ball or large festive gathering in crepe. Widows do not enter society for at least a year – that is, during the period of their deepest mourning.

People knew what to expect in Victorian times, and when they saw a young woman walking down the street, dressed head to toe in deepest black, they were less inclined to wander up and say something like, 'Feeling a bit better? You should get out more. Why don't you join the tennis club?'

It would be foolish to suggest that we should embrace the bleak, regimented mourning rituals of Victorian England, but overt displays of grief seem to have been replaced by covert grieving. In today's forward-thinking society you would expect widows and widowers to be treated with a modicum of understanding; but the reality of the situation is that society would rather not have to deal with us. In Britain today we have no way of displaying the depth of our grief. We choose not to adopt mourning dress, except on the day of the funeral; after that, black clothes stay in the wardrobe and we face the world in a riot of colour that belies the blackness and hopelessness that we feel within.

In Greek society, widows are revered, not reviled. Their plight is recognised; they are cared for, cooked for, and encouraged to express their grief openly. Black is seen as a mark of authority and there is no shame in wearing it. Keeping quiet and trying to be strong would be viewed with extreme suspicion in Greece, and perhaps we could learn a few lessons from the way that the women of the Mediterranean mourn. I'm not saying that we all have to go as far as wearing black for the rest of our lives, but a bit more wailing and groaning at the funeral, a bit more screaming and flailing, would mean fewer trips to the doctor and a lesser reliance on chemical stabilisers to restore our unbalanced minds.

In a world where people choose to wear ribbons on their lapels, signifying their support for all manner of charities and worthy causes, why do we choose to hide that which is making us sick and tired and socially unacceptable? A simple black ribbon would at least give people a clue as to why we are acting strangely, and looking so haggard and pale. It would give others a chance to prepare themselves to confront us for the first time; it would put words in the mouths of strangers and would negate the need for us to explain. But we can't do it, and so we hide our grief away, away from the outside world and away from polite society. We don't want to cause any upset and so we keep it bottled up inside; and when the words come tumbling out, they tend to do so only in the confines of the doctor's surgery – and all the doctor can do is give us 10 minutes of attention and a bottle of tranquillisers. But if the doctor gave us a black armband, or a black ribbon, then at least we could walk out into the waiting room, wearing – rather than bearing – the weight of our sorrow.

widowers and the conventions of mourning

Colliers Cyclopaedia makes no mention of widowers in regard to mourning dress – which is pretty staggering when you consider just how many social restrictions and regimented dress codes applied to a Victorian widow. It is purely a reflection of the way society viewed women at that time: women were dependent on men for their livelihood and social standing, and losing a husband would often result in total exclusion from polite society and complete financial ruin. Men were supposed to get out and find a new wife as soon as possible; they needed someone to run the household and bring up the children – the primary roles of a woman at that time.

There are many parallels that can be drawn from this with regard to today's social conventions, and I think it is true to say that, on the whole, widowed men tend to start looking for a new partner much sooner than their female counterparts. Despite all of the advances that have been made in the fight for women's rights, men still need women to fulfil the basic roles they always have done. Some men do stay at home to look after the children while their wives go out to work, but I'm sure if you asked them to choose between the role of homemaker and that of breadwinner, they would choose the latter every time. Many column inches have been devoted to the 'new man', and how caring, feminine attitudes are starting to infiltrate the mentality of today's modern male – but strip a new man bare and you will find there is still a trace of caveman lurking under his sarong.

David Robarts was 37 when his young wife Titania died, leaving him with four young children to bring up single-handed. I asked him for his view on why widowers tend to remarry so quickly. My rationale was that men have, by and large, a higher sex drive than women, and so need to find a regular partner quite quickly. And also that most men cannot cope with the home-making aspect of being a widower. This was his reply:

1. *Family – In my experience men who remarry quickly are often public school-educated career boys (my background, so not universal) whose wives were housewives. Therefore they have no experience of running a house and family. They flounder in the whirlpool of emotions, being unable to cope with theirs or their children's demands, and need to have a more permanent emotional anchor for themselves and their children, other than an au pair or nanny. Added to that is the cooking, cleaning and shopping, which is the equivalent of changing tyres, plugs and putting up shelves straight for most women – most men can't cope with the multitasking elements of it all and need a woman to straighten them out. Most men can't deal with the loneliness of bereavement and need companionship/looking after to keep them going. They find it impossible to communicate what they*

are going through to their male friends and awkward with their wife's female friends. They're supposed, I suspect, to rebound quicker and be out on the prowl sooner than a widow. They are likely to find someone to look after them and their family faster than a woman because they are ill-equipped to cope with all the shit that goes with running a job, family, house and social life. We rely on the wife to do it for us – sad but true!

2. Sex – Yes/no, again only personal experience, but it's not sex per se that is the driver. I haven't had sex for nine months but get by adequately on my own. Having said that, I'm gagging but am terrified of the prospect of being with another woman, paid or unpaid. I spent so long with Titania and have always been so bad at 'pulling' that to find myself on the market again fills me with dread. It's companionship that you're after, and not necessarily sex. We can all service ourselves quite happily one way or another, but to be able to have a cuddle or a hug or a non-conversational moment is the hardest part of all of this, and that is what men, I think, try to replace more quickly than women. Mainly it's an emotional void that we can't fill because we don't know until it's too late that we are missing it. Which leads me on to 3 . . .

3. Commitment – This is really radical but I think true. I don't believe most men commit themselves to the woman they marry as deeply as the woman does. I think there's a primeval urge to spread the seed and hunt the next orifice, and it's not until something fucking awful happens that we realise what we've got and what we've lost. That's not to say we all go and become serial philanderers, but that we don't show love and apprecia-tion for our wives. I think we take for granted so much of our women's being there, giving birth, looking after them, nappies,

homework, cooking our supper, cleaning our houses etc. that we lose sight of what matters. We get tied up in our lives and lose sight of theirs. Most men are selfish and have absolutely no idea of what it is like to run a family and don't want to. We love differently, and men in general are lazy about showing and appreciating what they've got, and therefore need to move on to do better next time.

But it all comes, ultimately, down to number one – we need to find someone to look after us because we are crap at looking after ourselves and revert to students.

The message regarding widowers in today's society appears to be essentially the same as it was at the turn of the last century – men have to get right back out there as soon as possible. It is their duty and their right, and if a man chooses to remarry within a year of losing his first wife, we should all feel grateful that he has found happiness in the midst of his grief.

> So much is expected of men; they are supposed to embrace their feminine side, but when it comes to showing grief they are expected to maintain a stiff upper lip and be strong for their own sake and for the sake of others.

It's easy to go to a pub or club when you're a single male – that's what single blokes do, isn't it? But what if they don't feel ready? Men are not heartless predators – they feel just as deeply as women. So what is a man supposed to do? Can he go to the pub and weep in front of his mates? Can he sit watching his children playing on the swings, quietly sobbing, while the bloke on the next bench tries not to stare? No, a man must be strong; a man must not cry; a man can go to the pub, but he must shrug off any outward signs of grief before he walks through the door. He'll get over it – he's a man, and men are so much better able to cope with grief than women.

Bollocks.

My message to people who think that men are tougher and braver and better able to cope with grief than their female counterparts is this: try kicking a man in the balls, and then get him to describe to you what it feels like.

He can't.

He might be able to mumble something just as soon as he's stopped feeling sick, but you'll never really know, because it's impossible for a man to tell a woman what it feels like to have testicles; and a man who has never been kicked in the groin is going to assume that his balls are tougher, and that he wouldn't have gone down so easily. Men will rarely be as open about their emotions as women because most men have been conditioned from an early age to hide all that mushy stuff away. But when a man finds a partner for life, he also finds an outlet for his deepest emotions, and is able – possibly for the first time since childhood – to express himself fully. Take that partner away and you also take away his ability to vocalise his most deeply held convictions, and to express himself honestly and openly without all the restrictions that society imposes. A woman is allowed to see things in her husband that he will keep hidden from the rest of the world. Take that woman away and you take away part of his voice, the part that speaks truly from his heart.

Richard Martin experienced a physical manifestation of his emotional turmoil:

I found myself reluctant to show my grief at times. For a man, old habits die hard, and this made the grieving process even more difficult. My grief exhibited itself in strange ways. Several months after losing my wife, whenever I felt at all stressed or emotional, I would lose my voice. My throat simply constricted until I felt I was choking and unable to speak. After a few minutes it would pass. I was convinced I had a medical problem, but my doctor assured me it was related to grief and would resolve itself. It eventually did.

So how do you cope? How do you allow yourself to grieve when the one person whom you can cry in front of is the one you're crying for? Well, I think there would be a lot of dignity in wearing a black armband. If you didn't want to talk about it, an armband would do all the talking for you. And don't be afraid to let others see you cry. I'm not suggesting that you go all soft and girlie; or that all widowers should retreat into the woods, get naked and engage in group hugging and hairy-arsed drum banging – just don't go all Victorian; don't shut down and pretend that it didn't hurt. It did hurt; it does hurt, so let yourself feel it. So what if society expects you to be a brave little soldier? So what if your friends have never seen you cry? Go ahead and cry – you'd cry if you'd been kicked in the balls, there would be dignity in that, so cry now – you're a widower and it hurts.

How should a widow behave?

Well, in these days of sexual equality and female liberation we should have left the constraints of Victorian society well behind – but sadly that is not the case. Widows are still expected to remove themselves from sight and from society until a suitable passage of time has elapsed. We do this, not just because society expects it of us, but also because we cannot face the prospect of having to socialise when we are being torn apart by grief. Self-imposed solitude is one of the few options open to us. But it could be worse

– we could belong to the Igbo tribe of Nigeria. If you think you've got it bad, take a look at what an Igbo widow has to undergo once her husband is dead (taken from a thesis by Chima Jacob Koreih 'Widowhood among the Igbo of Eastern Nigeria') . . .

An Igbo woman's first duty after the death of her husband is to drink the water that was used to wash his dead body. She must then scrape the hair off her head, as that is considered the crowning glory of the Igbo tribeswoman and must be removed in order to make the young widow appear ugly.

She is not allowed to bathe but can rub herself with sand if she needs to. She must eat off broken, unwashed plates and sit on the floor to signify her reduced status. She must sleep on the ground and leave the house only under cover of darkness. She must not talk to anyone or touch anyone as she is seen as defiled and capable of defiling others.

And lastly, she must weep on demand every morning for between three weeks and one year after her husband's death, whilst she praises him and laments his death.

In the central province of Cameroon, things aren't a whole lot better. The rite of widowhood starts with the widow lying flat on the ground for the duration of the funeral celebrations without being able to get up (this may go on for three days or longer). She must then roll in mud and then take hold of the trunk of a banana tree and, being careful not to trip or drop her load, she must then run and throw the trunk onto the road.

She is then anointed with palm oil and required to drink a mixture of various herbs gathered from the forest. Finally, she is allowed to return home, but not before receiving a number of blows to the head and body, administered by former widows.

If I were asked to choose between eating bridge rolls and talking to the vicar, and being rolled in mud and then beaten up by former widows, I have to say that I would choose the vicar every time. We should count ourselves lucky that we live in a society where we are allowed to fade into the background and not made a figure of public scorn, but that's not to say that our society doesn't find a way to exclude us. The methods are more subtle, and rarely involve banana trees, but they are often still painful and difficult to justify.

> A woman forms a tremendously strong emotional bond with her husband. She looks to him as her protector, as a provider and as the strength within the marriage. When he is taken away, a woman is left weak and exposed.

Most of us would be loath to admit it, but the Igbo tribeswoman is not a million miles away from the sophisticated, savvy woman you see in Waitrose, buying foccacia bread and quails' eggs. Take her husband from her and she will become as ostracised as an Austrian ostrich with Teutonic Tourette's syndrome and a scabious rash.

Your husband, the job he holds down, the house he provides and his circle of friends represent your social standing – take him out of the equation and you are left with a very vulnerable woman. I think if Charlie had been burned on a funeral pyre rather than buried, I might well have thrown myself upon it, if only to demonstrate the strength of my love for him. My problem as a widow was that I had no way of communicating the depth of my grief. Once Charlie had died, I was put in the 'widow' section of the general public, and given a finite time to get over the death of a man who had been my whole reason for living. I couldn't walk down the road in a bonnet of deepest jet, with black ribbons streaming behind me, trailing misery in their wake. I couldn't hide my trembling hands in a muff and rustle down to the village shop in a dress which screamed 'Damaged – stay clear!' I wasn't any different from everybody else – I looked the same, except for the black rings beneath my eyes. I was young and fit and healthy; I had to get back out there, get over it and get over myself. I could almost feel the clock ticking . . . Tick, tock, 'you should start getting out more – go to the gym, you'll feel so much better' . . . tick, tock, 'you should take a holiday' . . . tick tock, 'you must be over it by now' . . .

~

In summary

- There is no specific way to grieve.
- Consider wearing a black ribbon or armband as a way of preparing people for dealing with news of the death or your uncharacteristic behaviour.
- Don't feel self-conscious if you find yourself running screaming through the works canteen, or sobbing on the shoulder of the person sitting next to you in the bus queue. Grief cannot be hidden all of the time, and sometimes it will come bursting out of you at the most inappropriate moments.
- It's all right for a man to cry. It's not a sign of weakness to break down in front of people, so try not to bottle up your emotions to save the embarrassment of others.
- People will soon forget your loss.

8

the perfect diet

If you could patent it you would make a fortune – the only way to lose weight without ever having to try.

You will soon discover that weight will fall off you. Grief will suppress your appetite and render all food tasteless – that's if you can get anything past the big boulder wedged beneath your breastbone. If you loved cooking, as I did, and loved the fact that it made your partner happy, then you will never want to cook anything again – after all, where's the pleasure in cooking for yourself?

You have to eat, but your body will not demand to be fed. Your body will be silent while your mind tries to keep itself from breaking under the strain.

Death will make the Atkins diet a thing of the past.

You will no longer need a Slimfast shake to help you lose all those stubborn extra pounds. You have the perfect diet – a diet that doesn't cost you anything. Eat what you like beforehand; it won't make any difference. Soon you'll need a belt to hold up your trousers and a whole new wardrobe. Introducing 'The Dead Spouse Diet' – it's got a nice ring to it, don't you think?

So you will be slimmer but madder – Kate Moss on speed.

But it won't last – unless you let it.

coping with shopping

It will be difficult to visit the supermarket. Strangely, it was when I had to do the shopping for the first time that the reality of my situation finally hit home. It may well be the same for you, for while you are preoccupied with the funeral you will not really have time to think about what follows. Shopping takes thought; it will also take you past rows of razors, tampons, hairspray and aftershave, and when you see them, you will want to cry. Crying in Tesco's is a difficult thing, but it might stop you running down the aisles, tearing at your hair and screaming, 'Get that Brut away from me.' If you do this, people may get the wrong idea. So go ahead and cry if you feel like crying – they can't touch you for it.

It will take time to adjust to buying just for yourself, or for you and your children. It will take courage to enter the 'sad meals for one' aisle and fill your trolley. It is the first admission of being alone – and it will hurt. You are reminded at every turn that your life is now half of what it was. You see couples buying food together, you see women buying treats for their children, and men on their lunch hour buying bunches of flowers for their wives as a Friday night treat. You see what you can no longer have. You are in a vast room of memories that only you know the significance of. It's not a supermarket, it's a little shop of horrors.

I felt physically ill when I went around the supermarket for the first time. I didn't want to buy a small bag of potatoes – I wanted a big bag, for all of us to enjoy. I didn't want to buy only three carrots and a small lettuce – I wanted lots of food; food that used to keep Charlie healthy and happy, only he wasn't healthy any more and he would never again wake me up with a smile and ask if I wanted kedgeree for breakfast. So fuck smoked haddock; fuck beer and razor blades; fuck *GQ*; fuck tomato juice; fuck them all because they were no longer a part of my life. I was excluded from them now, and so I stuck to small things for three little people with not much appetite – inconsequential food, barely filling the bottom of the trolley. I couldn't face it; food was what made Charlie happy, food was what he cooked to make me happy. I'd lost Charlie. I'd lost my appetite. I wanted to fade away, to waste away – to be gone forever.

feeding yourself

You may have lost your appetite, but what happens when you regain it? Watching Nigella Lawson's graceful, grease-glistened fingers sensually dismember a soft-focus guinea fowl is a whole lot different from trying to follow one of her recipes. If you have never cooked before then you are likely to be in for a big culture shock.

First, what do you buy? Well, if you're not sure then it might be wise to ask a friend to accompany you on a shopping trip, and he or she will be able to tell you what you should have in your store cupboard. If you find that the whole experience is just too difficult to cope with then you might consider shopping via the Internet. Tesco's, Sainsbury's and Waitrose all have excellent sites, which will help to ease the pain of buying food. It may take a while to set it all up in the first instance, but once you have a list of essentials, reordering what you need each week will be a breeze.

If you have always left the cooking to your partner, and you want to try cooking for yourself, invest in a good, simple cookbook. You can't go wrong with saint Delia – her *How To Cook* book is a very good guide for beginners in the kitchen, as is *Jamie's Dinners* by Jamie Oliver.

You could survive on Pot Noodle and takeaways, but it is really handy to know how to make the basics, like white sauce and bolognaise sauce. If you can master even these two essentials, you will be able to make cottage pie, cheese sauce, moussaka, lasagne, chilli con carne and all manner of other dishes that will provide you with a good, nutritious diet. It will also give you something to make you feel good about yourself – you will probably not feel like cooking at all in the first few months, but if you do venture into the kitchen, you might find you learn to enjoy it. Cooking has many social connotations and is a really handy skill for anybody to have.

If you need a simple recipe to get you started, I'll give you one of mine. Now, when I tell people I'm making oxtail stew, they generally wrinkle up their noses because oxtail immediately brings to mind strong brown soup with tiny bits of mechanically-recovered meat floating just below the surface. This is different – this is hearty soul food, tender and succulent (imagine God squeezing a cow until all of the goodness and sweetness ends up in its tail). And it is guaranteed to make you groan with pleasure when you eat it ...

Oxtail stew with Madeira

olive oil

1 whole oxtail (any good butcher and most supermarkets
   can supply it), cut into small pieces

3 carrots, chopped into chunks

2 medium onions, roughly chopped

a handful of mushrooms

salt and pepper

a small handful of flour

a tablespoon of fresh chopped parsley, sage and thyme, or a
   pinch of dried mixed herbs

a good, big slug of Madeira

1 pint of beef stock or enough to cover the meat with half
   an inch of liquid

Take a large casserole dish and put in a good slug of olive oil.
Heat gently and, when the oil is smoking, put in the oxtail pieces
and fry them on all sides until nicely brown. When they are done,
remove them with a slotted spoon, put in the carrots and onion
and fry until edged with brown. Return the oxtail to the casserole
dish with the mushrooms, season well with salt and pepper and
sprinkle with a small handful of flour. Stir the meat around for a
minute or so to get the flour to swell, add the herbs and then pour
in a good, big slug of Madeira. Add the beef stock until the meat
is covered by about an inch of liquid. (At this stage, it will look a
bit watery, but after cooking all the liquid will have turned into a
lovely, rich gravy.)

Put a close-fitting lid on the casserole dish and put it into a
moderate oven for three-and-a-half hours.

Serve with mashed potatoes and peas and drink with a big,
bold red wine.

> If you cannot face cooking for yourself, and if people are kind enough to invite you out to eat in the early weeks, then try to take up their offer – even if you don't want to go out. But avoid dinner parties at all costs ...

a night to remember...

If I were asked to choose the single worst experience of my first month of widowhood it would have to be eating dinner with four married couples, three of whom I had only just met. It was excruciating.

You may find, as I did, that you say things that really shouldn't be said in polite company. This is because we all rely on our partners to give us a look when we have overstepped the mark. My husband wasn't seated opposite me, so I blithely launched into what I thought was a humorous story, but which ended not with a laugh but with a deathly hush, punctuated only by an occasional, 'Oh my God, that's really horrible.'

I wanted so much to be normal that night. I wanted them to like me. I wanted them to see that I was just like them. But I wasn't like them. What had come out of my mouth was only an expression of how mad with grief I was. I should have stuck a fork into my hand as an encore – I wouldn't have felt any pain, and the people around me would have been able to see that they were sharing a table not with a well-balanced but recently widowed young woman, but with a mentally unstable social liability.

You will say things you didn't mean to say. You will sit looking with envy at the affectionate glances that pass between couples. You will be subjected to stuttering sentences from people too frozen with embarrassment to know what to say to you.

You will die a thousand deaths.

So don't do it.

Visit friends in whose company you feel safe. Don't mix with strangers at this stage, because much as you think you might be ready to meet Mr or Mrs Right, you will be too mad to make rational judgements. And when you do go out for the first time, make sure you have a box of Kleenex in the car for the journey home. Because even if you have spent the whole evening laughing, when it comes to driving home alone it will hit you again. You have nobody to discuss your evening with and nobody to make you a cup of tea before bed.

You can't touch her.

He can't hold you.

There's a cold empty space beside you.

Now try to go to sleep.

In summary

■ Death will make you lose weight and lose your appetite. Food is a sensory delight, but you will temporarily lose the ability to derive pleasure from it.

■ Expect a trip to the supermarket to make you extremely upset.

■ If you cannot face going out, try shopping on-line, so you don't have to walk past all the things that remind you of the person you have lost.

■ Tell your friends that the best thing they can do for you is make you a meal, especially if you happen to live next door to Jamie Oliver or Nigella Lawson. Eating alone is one of the most soul-destroying things for a widowed person.

■ Making school packed lunches is tiresome and depressing, so try to do it the night before. Alternatively, if you cannot face it you could insist that your children eat school lunches, or put them up for adoption.

■ You have to try to eat because you will need to keep your strength up. Grieving can be exhausting and it is essential that you have the energy to cope with the physical and mental demands it will place upon you.

■ Don't accept invitations to dinner parties. Your grief will make you a social liability with strangers. Stick to the company of good friends.

9

sad, mad and dangerous to know: coping with grief

sleeping pills and antidepressants

You will almost certainly find that you need help to sleep. I found it impossible to sleep in the first couple of weeks and, much as I tried to avoid it, I had to resort to sleeping pills. I wasn't trying to be brave; I just don't believe in taking them. But I had to take them or else I would have collapsed, and when you have small children to look after you need all the help you can get.

The doctor will not give you a big bottle of pills because he will be aware that you might try to overdose. I certainly thought about it in some of my less lucid moments, until my doctor cheerfully announced that the ones he had prescribed were not good for killing yourself. Anyway, I told him I wasn't particularly bothered as I had a couple of shotguns downstairs, and because he was a good friend of mine, he knew I was only joking . . .

But I wasn't.

~

My experiences have taught me that you should think very hard before you start taking antidepressants. I'm not suggesting for a moment that you shouldn't take them if that is what you feel you need to get you over your grief. Your doctor will almost certainly offer them to you, and they will help you feel better. But let me tell you a good reason for not taking them.

Your grief, were it a purely physical symptom, could be seen as a large, black boil. You feel it constantly, and although others can't always see it, there it sits, festering under your skin. Now, you have a choice. You can either suffer with it every day, until it eventually bursts of its own accord and clears up, leaving you healthy and free of scars, or you can take a pill to dull the pain, allowing you to go about your daily business without the constant ache and occasional agony that the boil visits upon you. But the boil is still there, eating away at you beneath your skin. In it is stored all the anger, the hurt and the frustration you should be feeling, but the nice pill that you eat every day takes all that away. You may have a boil, but you are a smiley, happy, functioning individual.

And years later, when you decide to stop taking the nice pill because you are over the worst of it, the boil bursts and out will come every feeling you have ever suppressed, and all the grief you didn't allow yourself to feel because the thought of it was too overwhelming to deal with.

But you will deal with it now. It will hit you when you least expect; it will hit you hard and you may never recover from the shock.

the grieving process

I am not an expert in counselling or medicine, and I am not advocating ignoring the advice of a doctor. But you should realise that grief is a physical and mental process, which you have to go through in order to make yourself happy again. It is hard as hell – it is hell – and when you are going through it you think it will never end.

But there are ways of making it easier.

It will come over you every so often like a big black cloud, and it will weigh on you more heavily than anything you have ever experienced before. Turn a king-sized mattress into an overcoat and try walking around in it – that's what it feels like. You will be mad with it at times; you will scream and shout. If you have children, you will scream and shout at them all the time and hate yourself after they have gone to sleep. You will sink down under the weight of it and you will feel yourself suffocating, but you just can't get it off you. People will walk up to you in the street, but you will not be able to look them in the eye; you will only look down, because that is where you are. If anybody tries to be nice to you, you will feel your eyes welling up; if people are nasty you will want to scream at them, 'How can you say that? Don't you know what's just happened to me?'

I used to want to be pulled over by the police for speeding; I wanted a fresh-faced officer to lean into my car and say, 'Do you realise what speed you were doing?' And I would look at him and say, 'Yes officer, I do realise, now why don't you fine me – or better still, throw me in jail. In fact, why don't you just go ahead and hang me for being so reckless – you would be doing me a real favour because my husband's just died and I can't bear to be apart from him any longer.'

> Grief makes you quite, quite mad. But it does so for a reason — so let it.
>
> Be mad. Scream, shout, wail; embrace it.
>
> And when you think you are over the worst of it, it will hit you again.

I was driving my children home from a party one sunny afternoon in July, the car filled with the sound of my daughter's laughter, when suddenly, there in my head, was the noise my husband made when he was dying. It completely poleaxed me, and it was all I could do to drive home. I was dazed for the rest of the day and spent the night screaming and crying and shouting at the terrible injustice of losing such a wonderful man.

Why had my mind locked away that hateful sound, and then let me hear it again on such a happy day? Why? Because it wanted me to expel the massive hurt that was still sitting inside me.

mood music

You can prompt your grief. When you feel the cloud looming overhead, bring it closer, rather than trying to avoid it. Music is a powerful emotional cue, and you can use it to great effect. When you are sitting alone and depressed each evening, the songs you listen to will have the same, lasting effect as those you listened to when you were courting. You will probably identify with one particular song, which manages to sum up all you are feeling at that moment in time; and you will listen to it incessantly. Your mind needs this song because it is stimulating the release of your pent-up feelings, just as music can stimulate the release of endorphins when you are in a positive state of mind. Music will prompt you to feel all that your rational self is trying to hide. It will seep into your subconscious and free all those emotions you thought you had locked away.

Musical taste can vary dramatically – one person may cry uncontrollably on repeatedly hearing a ballad by Westlife – whereas I would have to be physically restrained from attacking the CD player with a baseball bat, but then we are all different. When I was grieving, songs by Radiohead made me feel especially melancholy, as did certain tracks by Elvis Costello and the jazz musician Chet Baker. I used to listen to albums by Eddie Reader and Everything But The Girl when I wanted to feel some sense of optimism about the future, and when I was driving alone and feeling in a 'Fuck you all, I don't care any more' mood, Nirvana at top volume provided a perfect accompaniment.

If I were to choose an album to grieve by now, it would contain the following tracks:

'Amsterdam' – Coldplay
'High and Dry' – Radiohead
'Nothing Compares 2 U' – Sinead O'Connor
'Everybody Hurts' – R.E.M
'This Woman's Work' – Kate Bush
'Achilles Heel' – Toploader
'Fake Plastic Trees' – Radiohead
'Far Away' – Carole King
'Say a Little Prayer' – Aretha Franklin
'Stay with Me Baby' – Lorraine Ellison
'René and Georgette Magritte' – Paul Simon
'Time After Time' – Everything But The Girl
'Home Again' – Carole King

'With a Song in My Heart' – Ella Fitzgerald
'Days' – Kirsty MacColl

Just as a note sung at perfect pitch can make a wine glass shatter, so a certain song can break through locked doors in your mind and trigger an outpouring of pent-up grief.

So listen. Listen to sad music. Look at old photographs. Bring it closer. Make it come over you, because each time you feel it, the next time you will feel it less, and in time you will hardly feel it at all.

they can't touch you for it . . .

I have received many e-mails since the launch of the merrywidow website on the subject of madness. Madness afflicts all grieving people at one time or another. It is nothing to be ashamed of – it is perfectly normal – but at the same time it is not something you can easily explain to anybody who hasn't actually experienced it. Madness can manifest itself in a variety of different ways, such as my desire to find a big brute of a man and use him sexually to the point where he was rendered incapable of decent walking. I also wanted to physically harm a number of individuals who had upset people close to me – and my defence would have always been the same: 'You can't touch me for it – I'm a widow.'

I felt at various times the need to kill myself, or walk out on my children and never return. But there was always a sense of responsibility, which prevented me from doing anything truly wild or reckless. When I look back on how I behaved, I think that my friends showed a considerable amount of patience with me, and the amazing thing was that they never made me feel like a freak because of the way I was acting. I mean, no girl in her right mind completes the 'Describe your best physical attribute' section in an application form from a respectable dating agency with the words, 'I've got a bum like a peach, only not as furry.'

Do they?

No, they don't – but I did.

Rebecca Chapman lost her husband in very similar circumstances to my own, and she wrote this:

> I had a hugely POWERFUL desire to shave all my hair off! I know it's a tradition in India with widows, but I never understood why. For me it was because I felt so altered inside and yet looked perfectly normal on the outside that I almost needed to make a physical statement by changing my appearance dramatically. I fought back the desire and didn't do it. I figured it would freak my kids too much, but then again they might have understood in their own way.
>
> I actually told my GP that I wanted to burn my house down because I was so fed up with everything (this was in the early days) – I just wanted to absolve myself of any form of responsibility whatsoever. She nodded sagely, and I don't think she wrote it in my notes!

Many people have written to me expressing the desire to cut their hair short, or even shave it off completely. One man who lost his wife in particularly tragic circumstances wrote to tell me that he had shaved off all his pubic hair. His wife had been ill for some time, and one of the symptoms was a complete loss of body hair. After she died, her husband felt the need to shave himself so that he could feel closer to her by feeling what she felt in the last weeks of her life. I think what he did serves as one of the most poignant illustrations of just how deeply a man can miss his wife.

Most people seem genuinely surprised when they realise they are not alone in becoming temporarily unhinged. Madness is the one thing none of us is ever prepared for. We see programmes about death; we know what is expected of us at the funeral; we know we are supposed to be strong, but madness is never mentioned.

So I'm mentioning it now. I want the world to know that I was as mad as a monkey with eight legs. I was certifiable. I was crazy; barking; bonkers; batty. But I was just a normal widow. I want you to know that it's alright to be wrong in the head; it's fine to be a fruitcake; it's perfectly acceptable to be socially unacceptable. Just try to be comforted by the fact that it won't last. We do and say dramatic things, theatrical things, unusual and startling things. We unmask ourselves. Our feelings vent forth and create havoc in the ordered, suppressed world that we inhabit. But we need to do it. We need to be mad; we need that madness to burst out and shock our dinner companions, or to prick the collective conscience of the hushed members of a kneeling congregation. We need death to show its face to all and sundry. We need to grieve.

But having said all that, we should beware of upsetting those closest to us during periods of madness, because it is very easy to alienate those you need most with a thoughtless word or gesture. We should always be aware of the feelings of others, even when the red mist descends. Grief is not an excuse for making others feel terrible, so please try not to take it out on those you love.

I'm not mad anymore – I'm still a bit scary, but I'm not mad. So please don't feel that by doing something that might be considered unusual or out of character, you are on the verge of insanity and therefore in need of a bit of electroshock therapy. Just do what you feel is right, what makes you feel better and more able to cope – just as long as it's not something really objectionable, like line dancing.

Madness and grief go hand in hand – and don't forget, they can't touch you for it . . .

Bling

I was thinking last night about a contingency plan for my dotage. I realise that if I don't find a suitable man with whom to spend my twilight years, then I'll have to find suitable employment to supplement my meagre pension. With this in mind I have decided to apply in advance for the job of village madoldlady. This would be the perfect way to spend my twilight years, and in the mental aptitude department I'm already halfway there. My village has only a small handful of elderly residents now. When I first met Charlie there were any number of nice old ladies and the occasional crone, but now the square is filled with affluent young families and an inordinate number of doctors. If you fall over and graze your knee on the street you suddenly become aware of doors slamming and bolts being slid home – our doctors are a reclusive lot.

The post of madoldlady is presently vacant, but the parish newsletter hasn't advertised for a new one yet. I think they must be struggling with a New Labour politically correct job description. What they need to be looking for is a wrinkly, bad-tempered octogenarian, with knobbly tights and only two teeth. They can't advertise for a toothless hag, because that would clearly upset too many people, so they'll probably have to ask for a 'non-gender specific orally-challenged

---

person of advancing years with anger-management issues and outstanding hosiery anomalies'.

There were some lovely old ladies in the village when I first met Charlie. There was the nice lady who lived opposite the village playground, who had a cockatoo and a large plastic donkey (but not necessarily in that order). The donkey stood outside her house with two potted geraniums in its plastic wicker panniers; the cockatoo sat in the window, and if you stopped to point him out to your children, the nice lady would come outside for a chat. I always thought it was a fine way to end up, standing by an ancient Aga, making cup after cup of tea, watching parents and children pass by and thinking about string theory (or in the old lady's case, wool theory).

In the house opposite lived a woman who was an example to us all. She reminded me of the star of *The Ladykillers*, but she was much more savvy, with twinkling eyes, a perky demeanour and a bright, enquiring mind. She drove an ancient Metro, and had the most spectacular garden in the whole village. Her garden was her passion, and her love of it was so strong that on warm summer evenings she would sleep out in it under the stars, and she continued to do this until well into her 90s.

The other old lady I clearly remember lived next door to us when we were first married. She was an altogether different proposition to the first two ladies. Her house wasn't neat and bright as a new pin, she didn't have a cockatoo or a plastic donkey; what she had was a crumbling, neglected pile and a crap-happy cat. I don't know what kind of person she had been in her prime, but in her later years she became as reclusive as Howard Hughes. Maybe she had her heart broken at a tragically early age. Maybe she had lost all her money on the gaming tables of some Monte Carlo casino. Who knows? But what was clear was that she was determined to spend her twilight years being exactly who she wanted to be.

We rarely saw her. Her house was ancient and dilapidated. It had once been the village brewery and had clearly been built to last, but now it looked tired and forlorn. Tatty grey net curtains hung limply from the windows and the house was only ever lit by a single bare bulb that shone feebly from the depths of the gloomy kitchen. A big, ugly cat used to sit in the window, and when you passed it would puff up its matted black fur as if to say, 'Tee hee hee. I'm going to have a really big dump in your rockery as soon as you leave for work.' We only saw inside the house once; there was a chimney fire raging and we were asked to help, so we crossed over into the dark side and stood in the kitchen, squinting in the gloom, trying to keep the lady calm while wondering how anybody could want to spend her twilight years in such desolate and tawdry conditions. But she clearly loved her house, and maybe she had so many memories of happier times that she couldn't bear to leave it. Perhaps she didn't need bright, clean walls and halogen spots; maybe she just needed her cat and a quiet life.

The lady only ever seemed to emerge from the house about once a week, when she would visit the post office across the square and collect her pension, or buy a tin of Happy Shopper cling peaches or a tin of cat food. But for all the shabbiness of her house, there was nothing unkempt about Mary. She would always step over her crumbling threshold looking her best, and it has to be said that Mary's best was an arresting sight.

Her look could best be described as Bet Lynch meets Miss Haversham. She strode from her cottage wearing a blue checked housecoat, looking for all the world like a cleaning lady from *The Mikado*. Her face was as smooth and white as a geisha girl's, with a layer of powder thick enough to coat every porcelain cistern top in Soho. Two large circles of rouge accented her cheeks; her lips were pink, and parted to reveal the kind of teeth that no peach in its right mind would want to cling to for long. She wore her hair in a high, backcombed bouffant, topped by a pink gauze chiffon scarf. But it was her accessories that really turned heads. Her eyes were hidden by a pair of sunglasses that Sir Elton John would have rejected as being too camp; they were big and pointy and ringed by diamanté crystals. Mary was blinging it for a whole generation condemned to a life of beige. Mary knew her look, and her look said, 'I'm not going to be drab, I'm going to sparkle. I'm beautiful and I want the whole world to see it.' I think she half expected to emerge on to the square to shouts of, 'Work it, girlfriend!' But all she ever got were curious stares and whispered asides.

Mary's gone now, off to spend an eternity sitting in the celestial salon of Mr Teesy-weesy, having a shampoo and set and skimming through the pages of *Picture Post*. So the job of village oddity is vacant and I think it's got my name on it. I never fancied spending my retirement dressed in mushroom and smelling like old wee, so I'm going to be an eccentric, I'm going to sparkle, I'm going to bling – I'm going to become a grandmofo with gold false teeth and a Thermos filled with Cristal. My invalid carriage will have 14-inch chrome rims and a plush red velvet interior. I will become P. Biddy, Gangsta Granny.

the side-effects of grief

Grief not only has a detrimental effect on your mind. A recent research study by a team of scientists from the University of Wisconsin has established a direct link between brain activity and immune function. Researchers have long known that psychological states like depression and vulnerability seem to be a trigger for a wide range of diseases, but now there is clear evidence to support that theory. But it doesn't take a learned academic to tell you that abject misery is often a precursor to ill health. Store it all up; store up all that grief and rage and misery and you can bet that it will soon manifest itself as an illness. This illness will not just be in your head; it will be seen by others, and in some cases it can be life-threatening. Your mind has the ability to heal your body when driven by positive thought, but it can just as easily leave you in a weakened and vulnerable state when it is besieged by negative emotions and depression.

There are countless books devoted to the power of positive thought; indeed, many people use visualisation techniques as a way to inhibit the spread of cancer. But if you turn your mind to black thoughts, and try to suppress your anger and grief by pushing them to the back of your mind and carrying on as normal, those black thoughts don't just evaporate. If the mind can be made to inhibit the spread of mutated cells then equally it must have the power to promote their spread. We should never underestimate just how powerful a force our emotions can be. If black thoughts were to manifest themselves on the surface of our bodies, like boils, you can be sure that we'd find a quick and effective way of dealing with them.

> The grief must be purged. You have to find a way to channel it out of you. Think of it as a temporary affliction and not a permanent feature of your life, and it will become just that.

Positive thought is all you need. You can resign yourself to being miserable for the rest of your life, or you can think yourself well. It will not be easy, and you will need a lot of help from your friends and family – but it can be done. Yes, it is painful; yes it is a long and difficult process, but so is chemotherapy. Which would you rather choose?

Try to remember that when you visit the doctor, you will be given between five and ten minutes of attention, and in that time your family practitioner is supposed to come up with an instant solution to a malady that may take years to overcome. You will walk out with a bottle of pills, but they are not the cure for what ails you – you are.

I cannot stress enough how important it is to grieve properly. It is terribly hard to have to face up to your deepest fears, but if you can find the strength to put yourself though it, you will come out of the other side a much stronger person. I know myself now. I know how strong I am. I know that nothing I face in the future will be able to defeat me because the death of a man I loved more than my own life did not defeat me.

Pills, or the power of your mind – I urge you to consider your options very carefully, and I wish you luck.

seeking help

I clearly remember a phone call I received following a disastrous visit to friends for the weekend. During the visit I had been shocked at the couple's treatment of me, and had left early on Sunday morning. Pretending to be normal and trying to stop my daughters' high spirits spoiling the newspaper-reading indolence of the other guests had proved too much to bear. I sent the couple a note on my return. Call it a cry for help; call it what you like, but for me writing, 'I'm drowning, and there's nobody to save me' was the only way I had of communicating just how desperate I felt. I think the couple were a little surprised to get my sad little communication among the other 'Thank you for a wonderful weekend' cards, but I've never been one to mince my words. The couple duly rang me to see how I was, but instead of the reaction I had hoped for, all I got was, 'I think you need to see a counsellor.' And there, in a nutshell, is the big dilemma that faces all widowed people: do we need to see a professional counsellor? And if we do, will it do any good?

I think counselling is entirely a matter of personal choice. I have heard from many people who have found great comfort after seeking professional help, but equally there are dozens of poor souls whose lives have been further tormented by the ill-judged comments and misdirected questions of certain 'professionals'. Charities such as CRUSE provide free bereavement counselling (www.crusebereavementcare.org.uk), but you may have to wait for months to get an appointment, and may decide that you would prefer to pay for a professional grief counsellor. There are several regulating bodies that govern counsellors, but membership is not compulsory. If you are considering paying for the services of a counsellor, you would be wise to check that he or she belongs to BACP (British Association for Counselling and

Psychotherapy, www.counselling.co.uk) or UKCP (UK Council for Psychotherapy, www.psychotherapy.org.uk), which are the two main regulating bodies for counsellors.

The problem with mental health professionals is this: if you do complain that your therapy sessions have been a total waste of time, isn't it your fault? It must be you who is blocking the treatment fundamental to your recovery; it must be your total inability to confront your grief that is hindering your counsellor's forward momentum. It's got nothing to do with the fact that the counsellor woman has no sense of humour, a serious moustache, and that her treatment room is drab enough to make even the most cheerfully optimistic client take a short walk to the refreshment trolley and overdose on non-dairy creamer.

Counselling is not always the answer. You can't expect all your troubles to be answered by a complete stranger, just because he or she is supposedly qualified to do so. If you cannot establish a connection with the person who sits opposite you, then you might as well be talking to a potted plant, or a stranger in a bus queue. You don't have to feel obliged to continue with treatment that is clearly having no discernible effect on your depression. If you feel that counselling is a waste of time, then you should exercise your right to choose either another counsellor, or another course of action. You should not be made to feel a failure because of your counsellor's inability to understand you and your emotional needs.

I have a good friend who is a counsellor. I have turned to her on a number of occasions and her advice has always been totally sound. In fact, if she weren't my friend I would gladly pay for her professional services, because her straight, no-nonsense approach is exactly what I need in times of crisis. What I don't want, I'm afraid, is what far too many bereaved people have to put up with – a whiney, depressing, socially inept, cardigan-wearing loser.

Having a beard and nodding a lot doesn't make you Sigmund Freud; it just makes you irritating. But many bereaved people feel that seeing somebody, however useless, is better than doing nothing at all.

My advice is this: only see a counsellor if you don't have any close friends you can turn to. Your friends, as I have already said, will be your salvation, and it is vitally important that you trust and respect the person you turn to for help in your hour of need. If you think group therapy is the answer, then by all means give it a try. Some people respond very well to being able to share their burden with others, and social interaction with sympathetic people could prove enormously beneficial.

If you cannot turn to friends or family for support, and don't feel able to face group therapy, then seeing a bereavement counsellor may be the right thing for you to do. You will hopefully establish an immediate connection with your counsellor, and find that the sessions are a wonderful way of releasing you from the burden of your grief. My rule for judging people in all walks of life is this: if they look you in the eye when they speak to you and have a sense of humour, then at least there is a basis for communication. If you feel you've had enough after a couple of sessions then so be it; you are the only person who is truly qualified to know what is best for you, so trust your instincts.

In summary

■ If you go to a doctor, you have to understand that you will get ten minutes of attention, which isn't nearly enough time for you to try to explain just how wretched you are feeling. The doctor cannot counsel you in that time; all he or she can do is offer antidepressants or sleeping pills.

■ Think very carefully about the long-term implications of antidepressant dependency before you embark on a course of treatment. Pills are easy to start taking but not quite so easy to stop.

■ Have faith in your ability to overcome your grief.

■ Don't be frightened of expressing your grief. Screaming, shouting and crying are all necessary ways of purging the hurt that you feel.

■ Don't suppress your feelings to save the feelings of others. Trying to be strong will only make you weaker in the long run.

■ Use music and photographs to prompt your grief; your pain is finite and each time you feel it, the next time you will feel it less.

■ You may feel that once you open up the floodgates and start crying you will be unable to stop, but you will stop. Fear of grieving is the greatest inhibitor of your ability to heal yourself. Your heart is already broken and crying hysterically will not damage it further.

■ Panic attacks and sleeplessness are both symptoms of suppressed grief, and if they continue over a long period of time your health may be permanently damaged as a result.

■ Don't expect anybody to understand just how desolate and devastated you feel.

■ Mourning is a lonely business, but it doesn't last forever.

- Don't expect a counsellor to be the answer to all your problems.
- When you are looking for a counsellor, make sure he or she is a member of either BACP or UKCP, the two regulating bodies for counsellors in the UK.
- Counsellors practise different techniques, based on what they have been taught, such as cognitive or person-centred therapy. The practices they employ will therefore vary considerably, so if one counsellor doesn't work for you, try another one.
- Try to find a specialist grief counsellor, but if you don't feel comfortable with your counsellor, or you don't feel any better after a few sessions, then exercise your right to go elsewhere.
- Don't forget that counselling can be expensive, but that the sympathetic advice of a good friend is free.
- Don't feel that you are a failure if counselling doesn't work for you.

10

anger management

One of the things that may come as a surprise to you as you emerge from the fog of confusion into the full-blown realisation of grief is how angry you feel. You will experience anger to varying degrees almost every day, and the focus of your displeasure will vary from small, mundane objects like the lid of a mayonnaise jar, to large and rather important objects like the Prime Minister or the school headmistress. There will be no set pattern for your bouts of rage; they will vary in length and ferocity and you may well feel a degree of guilt when they have abated – especially if you have just taken out your anger on your own children, as I often did to my eternal shame.

But why should you get so angry? Aren't you meant to be crying all the time? Isn't that what grieving people are supposed to do? Well no, actually you can do what the hell you like, and there isn't a single person on this earth who can tell you otherwise. I often took my anger out on my girls, and they were the only people who truly mattered to me at the time, so why was I making their life hell for a few minutes each day? The simple explanation is that we all need an outlet for our emotions, but when the need for an emotional outburst coincides with a loss of rational thought, the consequences can be rather alarming for those around us.

When you have found a partner for life, that person becomes the focus of all your love, your hopes and aspirations. You invest in that person, and the more you invest, the more love you produce, and hopefully, the more love you receive. Eventually, if you are lucky, you will reach a stage where you are totally consumed with love for your partner. You love unconditionally and are loved in return. This is what makes us truly happy. Money, big houses, manicured nails and fast cars don't make happy people – you only have to read the tabloid exploits of Robbie Williams and Geri Halliwell to see that. Loving another person and being loved in return is the one thing that no amount of money can buy.

But when that love is snatched away from you, when you no longer have a vessel into which you pour the best of yourself – a man to adore or a woman to worship – where does all that love go? You don't stop loving just because the object of your affections is dead. You still produce love for that person every waking moment, but you do so in the knowledge that they can no longer receive your love or give you anything in return. The love is trapped inside you with nowhere to go. It's not the kind of love you can give to your children or to friends; it is a special love – the very essence of all that is best in you. It is sex and sensuality; it is giving and laughing; sharing and learning. It is what makes us what we are as adults, it defines us in society, and life is pretty worthless without it.

It may take a while for your heart to recover from the emotional concussion, but once it does it is like waking up with the biggest, most throbbing hangover of all time. Out it pumps, all that love you feel. Out it pours, welling up inside you and washing around your chest, seeping down into your legs and up into your head. But you can't set it free, so it sits inside you, and slowly the deep, deep red of your love starts to take on a blueish tinge, and after a while it begins to harden and turn black. All that softness and lightness and joy start to atrophy; that spring in your step, which accompanied thoughts of your love, has gone. Your legs become leaden and the twinkle in your eye turns into a glassy stare. With no outlet for your hopes and fears, with no venting mechanism for your deepest emotions, the love you feel will turn into frustration and thence to anger. You have to get it out of you somehow, and the only way such a strong emotion can escape you is by coming out as pure rage.

You will feel rage all of the time, and at the most innocuous of things, but you must not think there is anything unusual in feeling anger. Love is the strongest emotion of all and is therefore potentially the most destructive if it has to be contained.

Grief will make you feel physical pain. Nobody tells you this. It cannot be written off as indigestion or heartburn. It is a physical manifestation of an emotional catastrophe and is your body's way of allowing you to feel the mental anguish bottled up inside you.

letting your anger out

As I have said before, the most damaging thing you can do when you feel frustrated and angry is to try and suppress it, either by taking tranquillisers or by locking it away and trying not to frighten the neighbours. Go ahead, frighten the neighbours; go outside and howl at the moon if that is what you feel like doing, just so long as you get it out of you. Society expects so much of us, but has no way of dealing with the grief of somebody who is in the full bloom of love.

If you need a way to vent some of your anger, I would suggest the following method:

Take one baseball/cricket bat, a sofa or large, comfy chair, and then look for a really banging tune (try to avoid anything by Sir Cliff Richard or The Swingle Singers). Turn up the music really loud and start to feel your emotions. Shut your eyes and try to bring forth all the suppressed rage you have been trying so hard to hold back. When you feel the rage welling up inside you, let it go by shouting at the top of your voice and beating the sofa or chair with the bat. Try to make sure there are no breakable objects or pets nearby, and really let rip.

The resulting soft furnishing injuries may necessitate a trip to Furniture Village, but it will do you the power of good and will hopefully negate the need for a trip to the funny farm.

Fruit

I'm scary; all my friends tell me so. I live at the end of a short lane, which is a good thing because it gives me distance from the rest of the village, and also gives people time to compose themselves before having to meet me. I don't know why people are scared of me, but I've got used to it now.

I've never met my postman as he won't come to the door. He stands at the top of the lane, folds my letters into paper aeroplanes and throws them at the house. The milkman has found a novel way of keeping his distance. He brings along a cow, gives it a sharp slap on the rump and sends it trotting towards the house. I get really fresh milk that way, but the milkman does find it rather awkward trying to fit the cow into a crate when it's empty. Even my friends find me scary, and I really can't understand why; it's bad enough having to be a widow, but being a scary widow just isn't any fun at all. I decided to ponder this problem yesterday, and found exactly the right diversion to help me think . . .

Alice decided to pull everything out of the junk chest in the hall. She was looking for her sunglasses, but instead she uncovered a whole heap of useless junk – single mittens, indoor boules, torn swimming hats, bits of string and broken water pistols. I put all the junk in a bin bag, but I couldn't throw away my favourite jigsaw puzzle. It was sitting at the bottom of the chest; it was speaking to me; it was saying, 'Look at my fruit bowl; admire my crusty loaf. Make me, Kate, you know you want to . . .'

Lots of adults do jigsaw puzzles, don't they? Admittedly, most of them are either senile or in restraints, but even so, if an incontinent axe murderer can find peace and contentment with a jigsaw puzzle then so can I.

The pieces were a lot smaller than I remembered, and there were so many of them, mostly with the same pattern. But it was easy when I was a girl, and now I'm so much older it should be simpler, but my eyesight is worse, my knees hurt and my neck aches – but I kept on thinking, 'I'm going to do this; I'm going to do it for Alice.'

I had to find all the edge bits so I could give Alice an easy framework to start with, and as I was doing it I thought, 'I'm not that scary. I don't sit at the window and scowl at passers-by – I kneel on the floor, getting leg cramp and eye strain, and all for the benefit of my daughter.' That's not scary, that's devotion.

An hour later and I was still trying to get the outside of the jigsaw in place, and when I'd finished there was a worrying number of pieces left over. Still, that was the hard bit done, and now I could give my knees a rest and get back to writing my journal . . .

My goddaughter has landed a part in her school musical – she's playing a prostitute. Her mother is accepting the role with characteristic pragmatism; I'm very proud but at the same time I am rather hoping she doesn't show any aptitude for the job. At least the part of a prostitute is one up on the role I had to play at my school's production of *Wind in the Willows*. I was overlooked for any of the major roles, and was left with the job of playing the simple but obliging carthorse. I think my only line was, 'Climb aboard, Mr Toad, and I'll give you a ride,' which, in a strange way is not too dissimilar to Annabel's opening line of, 'Hello dearie; fancy a good time?' I wasn't too badly scarred by the experience, so I'm sure my goddaughter will be fine.

Back at the jigsaw puzzle, and I still can't find all the bits of strawberry, and do you know what I say? I say, 'Fuck it.' Life's too frickin' short to spend three hours on your knees, squinting at tiny bits of cardboard that don't even fit together properly. I don't know what I was thinking when I was a teenager – I should have been snogging some pustulant boy in the village bus shelter, instead of spending my time hunched over a table, trying to piece together a bowl of fruit and a crusty cob. Maybe that's why I've turned out the way I have. I was a sad teenager and now I'm a scary adult, and it's all the fault of the frickin' jigsaw . . .

I can't do it any more. It's too hard and too fiddly and too boring, and why the hell am I wasting my time engaging in a pastime for shut-ins and spinsters? I should be out in my lane, shouting at passing cars, scratching myself and looking deranged . . .

Alice came home from school a short while later and the jigsaw was back in the box. Hell is a world made up of 2,500 tiny pieces. I had spent the day in terrible torment; I couldn't put her through what I'd just been through and so the jigsaw had to go. The still life of fruit and comestibles is now being pondered over by a little old lady in the British Heart Foundation charity shop. She's wondering why the box is so battered and some of the bits have been chewed, and why the woman who brought it in had the look of a deranged axe murderer . . .

The other notable event that happened this week was my attendance at a first aid class. I definitely lost points for trying to French kiss the resuscitation dummy, but I managed to score highly on the 'Response' section by suggesting that prodding the victim with a stick would be a good way of checking for signs of life. I could have happily prodded my first aid partner with a stick – he had cold, clammy hands and I really didn't appreciate them being run all over my face. Still, I'm all set to go out and do good, so if you should happen upon a man lying on his back with a gleeful woman sitting astride him giving him completely unnecessary mouth to mouth, you'll know it's me.

11

how can you help your children?

Coping with your own grief is hard, but it is nothing compared to dealing with the grief of a child. What you do and say to your children in the early weeks and months will help to shape who they are, but also has the potential to damage them for the rest of their lives.

a picture of grief

Young children do not have the capacity to vocalise their emotions, so you have to give them a way to tell you how they feel. The best way to do this is by stapling a few pieces of paper together and giving it the title, 'A book about how I feel about my mummy/daddy'. Tell your children that they can draw in the book whenever they feel sad about mummy or daddy. I did this with Rosie and was amazed at the pictures she produced. It is hard to see your child drawing pictures about death, especially when he or she skips home from playgroup with a big painting of a graveside scene, but you have to understand that it is the only way children have of telling you how they are coping, and if all the people in the picture are smiling, then you know that you are doing something right.

lead by example

Children learn by example. You must let them see you cry, and in that way they will know it is all right for them to do the same. I have a friend who was told by her stepmother that she could not cry when her father died. She was only nine years old, and that part of her emotional psyche shut down from that day onwards. She found that she could not allow herself to release any sadness. She never cried; her sadness was stored inside her and the frustration of keeping it there came out as anger. She was so angry as a child that she used to pick fights with the large Alsatians that roamed her estate. She wrestled them, and she won. It has taken years of counselling for her to be able to release what her stepmother made her lock away. But it was her stepmother who should have been locked away.

That is an extreme example. Not all children have cruel stepmothers – some have loving mothers or fathers who simply cannot allow their children to see that they are sad. Perhaps the most damaging thing for a bereaved child is never being allowed to talk about his or her parent's death.

> If children cannot mourn properly, they will spend
> their adult life trying to recover from the emotional
> scarring – and some people find that they never
> recover.

As children grow older and learn more about the world around them, their capacity for understanding and perception of others increases, and allows them to mature emotionally. All this will continue over time, and with the benefit of a stable, loving environment, they should turn into happy, well-balanced adults. However, if a child is faced with an emotional trauma that he or she is unable to fully comprehend, and is not given sufficient help from an adult to deal with that trauma, then the child will go into 'emotional lock-down'.

Take the example of a young boy who feels unable to talk about the death of his mother. Just because he cannot express his pain verbally, it doesn't mean he isn't hurting. If he sees his father being strong and silent, then he will almost certainly follow his example, even if it feels wrong. Unresolved grief is like radioactive material – a glowing rod of plutonium in the mind of a child. The boy doesn't get a mental lead-lined box for complex emotional issues until he's an adult, so all he can do is lock the hurt away in a room in his head and try not to think about it. He will shut the door, because locking pain away is a child's way of coping. But, just as plutonium emits damaging radiation, so the pain will seep out, out through the walls and under the door of the little room in his head, and over the years it will affect almost every aspect of his emotional life. And when that boy reaches adulthood, he will finally understand the true nature of what he has been carrying around wordlessly for years – but by then it will almost certainly be too late. The hurt that was locked away is still locked away in the mind of a child. The room is now a glowing, poisonous danger, but the man knows that if he opens the door, it is a frightened little boy that will have to deal with the consequences.

This is an extract from an e-mail I received from a man who asked to remain anonymous. This man is still deeply troubled by the events that took place after the death of his father.

I lost my father when I was six years old. My mother came to school with my younger brother to collect me. I remember sitting on the headmistress's office floor playing with my brother while my mother talked to the head. When we left the school my mother told me that my father had died. I hadn't even known he was ill and in hospital; I thought he had been at work all the time. I can't remember how I reacted at the time but it affected me for years. My school work suffered badly, I became introverted and developed serious health problems which plagued me until adulthood. There was no form of counselling and it seemed that we just had to get on with it. I can remember some time later sitting in the front room at home and watching my father cycle past without stopping. I guess I just didn't accept that he would never come home again. My mother did a great job as a single mum, even though I can remember going through some pretty tough times. I don't think she received any help, counselling or advice.

I have always felt there has been a hole in my life from not having my father, and I certainly didn't know how to be a father myself. I'm 52 now and still feel emotional when I think about it; just writing to you makes me feel very sad. If there is any way to help children who lose their father, then it must be done so that they can grow to be normal, balanced adults. I'm not sure if I am.

That e-mail serves as a stark and poignant illustration of just how deeply the loss of a parent can affect a child, and of how long the effects can be felt if not properly dealt with at the time. The man who wrote it was adamant that I use his words, in the hope that others might not spend the rest of their lives suffering as he has. Many men have since written to me to tell me about how the death of a parent has blighted their adult life. One man believed he would die young because his father did. The death of his father was not discussed within the family and so the fears of a small boy have become the neuroses of a grown man.

Another man wrote to tell me of the anger he directed towards those he loved. He was wracked with guilt, but felt that if he tried to release all of the grief he was suppressing, he would never get over the shock. He said, 'I want so much to cry, but I know that if I start, I might never stop.' A grown man was telling me that he wasn't strong enough to cry, but he was telling me in the voice of a frightened little boy – a little boy who was still clearly suffering.

be open

Openness is imperative. Most people will find it unnerving if your child talks openly about death, but you should never discourage a child from being open and honest to save the embarrassment of an adult. Rosie would walk up to total strangers and tell them that her daddy had just died, which, to a four-year-old girl, seemed a perfectly natural thing to do. Some of the people she spoke to were amazingly kind and some just couldn't think of anything to say, but the point is that she felt able to express herself. She had a little more difficulty at school, because although her teachers were very patient with her, there was only a certain amount of attention they could devote to an individual child. It was only when I was called in to see Rosie's headmistress and form teacher that I knew she was getting into trouble. She was clearly trying to get attention and couldn't understand why she was being punished for doing so. She was also being taunted in the playground, which is a standard reaction to a child who is seen to be 'different'.

Young children cannot dress up what they are feeling with artifice and invention – they just come right out and say what's on their mind. My daughter often found comfort in the words of her classmates, but more often than not she would come home in tears because somebody in the playground had been cruel to her. There is nothing you can do to protect your child from being hurt at school. All you can do is offer comfort and reassurance at home and try to explain the reason why other children say hurtful things.

dealing with teachers

School teachers are not usually given any formal instruction on how to deal with a grieving child, and so the reaction your child's grief can provoke in his or her teacher can vary dramatically. Your child's school may decide to send the teacher in question on a counselling course, but I think such schools are an exception. Teachers have quite enough to deal with on a day-to-day basis, so it will be up to you to give your child's teacher guidance.

In Rosie's first year of school I made the mistake of assuming that everything was fine because she wasn't telling me about the trouble she was getting into. I should have gone to see her teacher and asked about her progress every couple of weeks, so that I could have been made aware of any problems and addressed them long before they became a serious cause for concern. But equally, Rosie's teacher should have approached me as soon as she noticed that Rosie was behaving in a disruptive manner, as it was so totally out of character.

Communication is the key, but it's hard to walk up to a teacher in the playground when you can hardly bear to leave the house. It takes cooperation on both sides, and your child's teacher must understand that the grief of a child is an ongoing issue, not one that can be forgotten after a couple of weeks. Difficulties at school will compound all the problems you will experience at home, but it is vital that you communicate with members of staff and make them aware that your child may need to be shown patience and compassion long after it is deemed necessary to treat him or her like the rest of the class.

your child's grief – an ongoing process

Some of the most remarkable people I know lost a parent when they were young. Children will find strength of character that will last the rest of their lives, if you only give them the chance to look inside themselves and discover it. And if you try to stifle that need for self-enlightenment – if you keep them in the dark – then that darkness will overshadow everything they try to achieve in later life. So let them go to the funeral if they ask to do so; let them talk until they have exhausted all of their questions, and if all they do is ask the same question a hundred times over, then you must answer it a hundred times over.

> Your child's grief will not necessarily coincide with your own – it may come out a year or so later.

If your child begins to display uncharacteristically antisocial behaviour, as my own daughter did, then you have to realise that he or she is doing so to provoke a reaction. If all you do is get angry, as I did, then you are not seeing what they are trying to make you see.

It took a friend to open my eyes and make me realise that Rosie was crying out for my undivided attention. She wanted to be treated as an individual; she wanted me to stay with her as she fell asleep each evening – she wanted to be made to feel special. It was so easy to remedy the situation: I took her 'girlie' shopping, we had lunch out together and we talked about her daddy. It was difficult at times; she was so preoccupied with Charlie that she would walk into shops and say in a very loud voice, 'What was I doing when daddy was dying? Was I the one who was laughing, or was I crying?'

But I couldn't stop her and I would have been wrong to try. She was just a little girl, struggling to come to terms with the death of her daddy. It took a while, but we eventually got through it together, and if I hadn't been made to see what I was doing wrong, I might have ended up with a different and difficult child, instead of the balanced and loving daughter that I have now.

There is no magic formula when it comes to knowing the right way to bring up your children single-handed. All you can do is try to do what you feel is best for them; try to carry on instilling in them all of the values that were important to your partner, and try not to be too hard on yourself. There is no good cop/bad cop routine – you have to be the bad cop all of the time. You will get tired of being hard on your children in the absence of a moderating voice, but as long as you show them love and understanding they will not resent you for it.

Older children

As children reach adolescence the problems become altogether different. Dealing with adolescents can be so much harder than dealing with small children; a hormone rush coinciding with the shock of losing a parent can be devastating to any young person. For a young man, losing your father means losing your role model. Girls are often idolised by their fathers – to lose a man who saw you as his princess can be a crushing blow to somebody who is just blossoming into womanhood. And when a mother dies, the core of the family is lost and the impact her death has on the rest of the family can be absolutely catastrophic.

Teenagers are stuck in an emotional twilight world between adulthood and childhood. They want to be seen as adults and crave independence, but need the same level of emotional support as children. In fact they often need more support, because to compound the problems of emotional immaturity, teenagers also have exams, spots and myriad other problems to deal with. A 16-year-old girl who has lost her father is still too young to shoulder the burden of her own grief, but is old enough to be aware of the emotional needs of her mother and younger siblings. She will try to be strong for her mother and the rest of the family, but at the same time will be desperate to lean on her mother for comfort and reassurance. She will invariably hold back her tears to save upsetting those around her, but this need for self-control could trigger a whole host of associated problems, such as allergies, bulimia, anorexia and self-harming. It is no good expecting a teenager to let you know how he or she is feeling; you have to take control of the situation and provide the example for your child to follow. I know this will be extremely difficult for you when you are struggling to deal with your own grief, but you have to remember that your actions will lay the foundations for the future happiness of your children. Get it right, and you will be giving a teenager the very best start in life. Get it wrong, and you will spend the rest of your life dealing with the consequences.

I received an e-mail from a young woman who was worried about her brother and the effect his bad behaviour was having on his grieving mother. The family of six had only recently lost a father; the mother was showing her grief by shouting all the time; and her 14-year-old son was doing everything he could to disrupt the rest of the family by refusing to comply with every instruction given to him. I am not an expert in child counselling, but I could see the problem lay with a lack of communication. How is a young man supposed to let go of his grief over the death of one parent if he cannot confide in the other? If all he ever hears are barked instructions then he is bound to rail against the woman with whom he is trying so hard to communicate. The boy was obviously being disruptive to get his mother's attention, but it was a fruitless act under such tense circumstances.

I could understand why the mother was so angry; after all, she had been left to bring up five children on her own. She was fortunate to have such a caring daughter, who understood the need to seek advice about the situation at home. I suggested that she should sit down with her mother and brother and try to talk calmly about what each of them needed. You cannot find a solution by shouting at the protagonists and expecting them to comply. What was clearly needed was a controlled discussion, where each person was given time to speak and where nobody got angry or refused to hear the opinions of the others. The girl took my advice and sat down and had a quiet talk to her mother. I think it has been the starting point for the family to work together and try to find an understanding of each other's needs.

Sarah Snaydon, a mother of two teenage girls, wrote this:

the pan? I feel that emotional stability is the key to being able to move on and try to live a normal life. If you try to push a child's grief to the backburner while they take their exams, you are storing up trouble for the future. They may well have the qualifications, but they will lack security and may feel real anger that they were not allowed to grieve. Having said that, it is very hard to resist being uptight about school work. You do feel anger that, as well as losing a parent, they are also losing out educationally – as if the one wasn't enough. Unfortunately, an emotional trauma and a failure to achieve potential are bedfellows.

Counselling will help some teens – but only those who like to talk. Rachel is a naturally open and gregarious person. She had regular counselling and I'm sure it helped her. Katie didn't want it initially and is only now coming round to the idea that it might help her, though she's still not keen. You can't make your children grieve in the way you do – and you can't make them grieve at all if they're not ready. All you can do is be alert to obvious cries for help such as self-harming. Other adults were horrified, and some almost disgusted, by the fact that Katie was cutting herself. I realised there was nothing I could do to stop it and just tried to get her to open up to me. I can't understand what she feels when she does it, but I realise it's one way of making an unimaginable pain feel real. Teenagers are typically full of self-loathing at times too, and I think this is a related manifestation.

Most days, like their parent, teens will just get on with life. But when I find myself thinking about Geoff and what I've lost in most waking hours, I guess that they are doing the same and we are all ploughing a grim furrow together. But that last word is the key – together. Although your loss is different – and when they find their partner, hopefully their grief will be tempered – you are sharing the experience of trying to cope with it.

Hurdles like leaving home will turn into Beechers Brook, and every family joy will be tinged with sadness that daddy isn't there to share it. As you say, they are terrified of losing the other parent. Rachel was horrified to hear that I was going to be using the Tube in London – I think she was convinced I'd be the latest victim of the terrorists. What can you do? I don't believe that lightning doesn't strike twice – neither do they. All you can try for is to keep grounded in reality, and recognise that you – and they – are bound to get some things out of perspective. Keeping a sense of humour is important too, and just giving them all the love that you can. Just because they are down to one parent doesn't mean that they go short on the love stakes – my family, Geoff's family and above all I, can keep the glass full.

providing reassurance

For any child, one of the most obvious effects of losing a parent is the fear of losing the one that remains. Your children may feel desperately insecure, not necessarily all of the time, but you may well notice they occasionally become very emotional and clingy, and seek constant reassurance from you. Any illness you suffer, however slight, may strike dread fear into your children, and so it is vital that you are aware of how your health will affect their emotional stability. You may have to give your children a great deal of love and reassurance to allow them to overcome this chronic insecurity, but it is vital that you do so.

My children occasionally get very upset at the thought of me dying. Even though I am at pains to tell them that I am fit and healthy, if I do get a bad case of flu, they both think they will end up as orphans. So I sit with them both on my lap, I cuddle them and I tell them that I am not going anywhere. I tell them that God put me here to take care of them both, and so that is precisely what I intend to do. I tell them that they can live at home until they are 60, if that is what they wish to do. I give them every assurance they need to make them feel happy and secure, and I do it over and over again until I am sure I have allayed their fears. But I know that as soon as I get another cold, a germ of an idea will start to grow in their heads and I will have to reassure them all over again.

All children really need is time, patience and love. You *can* sit and cuddle a 17-year-old boy; just because he's six inches taller than you doesn't mean you can't give him a hug when you think he needs one. Give your children hugs and kisses and love and understanding and you can do no more.

getting help

Sometimes you may feel that your love is not enough. If you think your child needs to see a counsellor, then you must also ask yourself why. Consider the need for you to see a counsellor yourself before you put your child through that process. Your child may be desperate to talk to you, and may well start to become withdrawn or antisocial as a way of drawing your attention to the problem. It is easy to get into a cycle of non-communication; you will not cry in front of your child for fear of upsetting him or her, and in the same way your child will think that he or she cannot let you witness any sort of emotional outburst for fear of making you upset too. As I have said before, if you lock away your grief from each other then you will set a pattern for later life. A boy who goes quiet when he's upset and retreats to his room, rather than talking to his mum, will invariably grow up into a man who cannot share his feelings with his wife. And it is not good enough to say, 'He does that – he's just like his father.' Why can't a mother talk to her son about his problems, simply because she could never communicate with his father on a deeply emotional level? Do men always have to be seen as strong and silent? We have to be mother and father to our children; we cannot hope to replace what has been lost, but we must strive to forget our own problems and look to their future happiness. So listen to your children; don't shut down because you are dying inside. Try to talk and not to shout. Open up to them, and give them a chance to open up to you.

You are the key.

But what if you can't cope? If you really feel you are unable to give your child the level of understanding he or she requires, then by all means seek outside help. There are many fantastic organisations that have been set up specifically to address the problems of childhood bereavement. I know from the mail I have received on the subject that such charities can make a real difference to the lives of children who have lost a parent. Children and young adults who have suffered a loss are brought together and encouraged to work through their grief, while being supported by their peers. Counsellors employ several different techniques, including art and drama therapy, which help children to express grief in a safe and happy environment. It is a wonderful thing for young people to be able to talk openly about their emotions and experiences, without feeling they are upsetting anybody. Children need the reassurance of their peers, and I can think of no better way to help a child.

The details of the charities devoted to helping children cope with the loss of a parent can be found at the back of the book.

In summary

- Children do not properly understand the concept of death until they reach about six years of age.
- A young child may seem perfectly accepting of his or her parent's death, but sooner or later the full realisation of what has happened will hit home, and this is the time when you will have to employ all your powers of understanding.
- Encourage your child to draw pictures to illustrate how he or she is feeling and make a special book for these drawings. It will give your child an emotional outlet vital to recovery. The pictures may be graphic and upsetting but they will be the best illustration of unspoken grief and provide you with a valuable insight into your child's emotional well-being.
- Do not expect your child's grief to coincide with your own; it may take years for the grief to come to the surface.
- Uncharacteristic or antisocial behaviour is a sign that your child is trying to get your attention. It is a cry for help. Children are emotionally immature and do not possess the skills to vocalise their feelings properly.
- If you have more than one child then it is vitally important that you try to give each child some time when they get your undivided attention. Your children will feel especially vulnerable and needy, and giving them one-to-one attention will help make them feel secure.
- Be prepared for your child to get a rough ride at school. Other children can be especially cruel and there is nothing you can do to shield your child against playground taunts.
- Don't expect a teacher to be fully sympathetic to your child's grief. Teachers don't have much time to devote to the needs of individual children and it will be up to you to monitor your child's progress at school and flag up any potential problems that might arise.

■ My children love to tie messages to their daddy onto helium balloons and send them up into the sky. In this way they feel able to communicate with their father, and it makes them feel special.

■ Making a box of memories will help your child express his or her feelings and will also provide a focal point when your child feels sad. The box can contain photographs or mementoes, bits of cloth, jewellery or anything your child associates with his or her parent. Writing down memories and putting them in the box will also help your child.

■ Never stop a child expressing grief to save the feelings of an adult.

■ Talk about your late partner as often as you can, and let your children ask as many questions as they like. Knowledge about a dead parent will help your children come to terms with their loss.

■ A teenage child will suppress grief to save hurting your feelings, but this can be hugely damaging in the long term, so it is up to you to let your son or daughter know that they will not be upsetting you by crying or shouting.

■ Suppressed grief in a teenager can lead to a whole host of associated problems, such as eating disorders, allergies, addiction and self-harming.

■ The pressures of exams and puberty will compound the pain of grief in a teenager; this is an explosive combination and if you ignore the danger signs then your child could end up with permanent emotional scarring.

■ There are many wonderful organisations devoted to helping children who have lost a parent, so consider seeking outside help if you feel unable to cope.

■ Show your child unconditional love and understanding: talk, listen, understand, and you can do no more.

12

being strong

If there is one theme that runs throughout the mail I have received since setting up the merrywidow website, it would have to be strength. Strength is something people expect you to have, but it is the first thing that leaves you when you lose your partner. People will tell you that you are strong because that is what they want you to be. If you are strong, you are coping and you will get over it – you won't need the help of others and that is what others want. But what is strength? If we are talking about self-belief and fortitude, then I think I can safely say that the recently bereaved lack any notion of either. When you have a partnership, your self-belief is buoyed up by the belief your partner has in you. If you are told every day that you are clever and attractive, witty and kind, then you will believe it and you will become it, even if the rest of the world sees you as a complete dolt. You reflect what the eyes of your lover see in you. You become a better person because of their attentions and their compliments.

A good partnership is about loving yourself, as well as

another person. When your partner dies, all of your past achievements, your shared experiences, your secret jokes and fond remembrances die too. All of the confidence that another person had in you suddenly evaporates; with it goes your self-belief, and what may have taken years to accumulate will dissolve in a matter of seconds. You will suddenly start to question your ability to do even the most simple of tasks because you have no emotional backup if you fail. You will be plagued with self-doubt, but because you know you have to carry on, others around you will assume you are feeling strong and assured. People want you to be strong because it means you are coping. They want you to say 'I'm fine' when they ask you how you are, because it will bring the conversation to a neat little end and everyone will walk away feeling happy – everyone except you. You couldn't even begin to explain just how wretched you are feeling, so to spare the feelings of others you deny your own; and so begins a cycle of opening up and locking away.

When you are alone, watching television or listening to the radio, something will invariably trigger an outpouring of grief. Corny lines that would normally have been laughed off take on a huge emotional significance. Anything remotely connected with happiness or romance, with death or loss, will become a cue for tears. Men and women will react the same way, regardless of how 'strong' they are perceived to be by the outside world. But when you go out in public, when friends come round to see you or meet you in the street, you have to shut away all of what you feel, and you do it for their sake, not your own.

> You will become strong again, but only after you have been through a most testing and tortuous ordeal.

It is important to understand that you are weak, vulnerable and exposed, and that only time and the recovery of self-belief and self-worth will make you feel stronger and better able to cope. You will need people around you to give you strength, not platitudes. Draw on them when you are feeling weak; draw from them hope and optimism. Hug them when you feel the need for physical closeness and cry with them when you feel alone. Use them because you cannot get through this by yourself.

Strength will return to you slowly, and there will be many tears before you feel brave enough to stand up and face the world again as a fully functioning individual. There is no secret formula I can give you, but what I can say is that each time you complete a task you would have normally left to your partner, you will have taken a single step closer to being able to cope with life without them.

Small steps and time; your strength will return to you, but instead of being dependent on another person for reassurance, you will know in your heart that you have the ability to do anything you set your mind to. That kind of self-belief is something so many people spend a lifetime trying to attain, and it will be yours if you just have the courage to believe you can survive alone.

In summary

- People will say you are strong when you feel at your weakest.
- You will try to be strong for the sake of others.
- Believe in yourself. Weakness is not a weakness when you have lost your whole reason for being.
- You really are strong, you just don't know it yet.

13

the loneliness

All that crying and shouting certainly takes it out of you, doesn't it? But at least you can have a bit of peace and quiet at the end of the day. It's nice, that time by yourself, isn't it?

Isn't it?

One of the most laughable things that happened to me after Charlie died was that I found myself looking forward to being able to watch films by myself. I know I wasn't right in the head, but I am ashamed to say that it did cross my mind how great it would be to be able to watch some of the movies I knew Charlie wouldn't enjoy. I thought to myself, 'I can watch what I like now. I can cook something delicious, open a really good bottle of wine and sit by myself in peace and quiet.'

Now how much fun was that?

Not much.

The feeling of liberation lasted for a couple of nights, and then the loneliness set in. The longing that I felt for his touch and his smell and the sound of his voice gnawed away at me. I didn't feel him. I felt nothing. I had an insatiable hunger, a thirst that could not be quenched. All of my senses cried out for some cerebral response, but there was none. I was empty.

Empty and alone.

All the love that had filled me up and consumed my every thought and deed had been replaced by emptiness. Inside me was this thing; this being; this black, miserable, sucking entity, which swallowed up every pleasurable experience that might have brought me some kind of solace or enjoyment. It sucked away at me, this dark vortex. It sucked at my hope, my resolve and my optimism, and spat out despair. I couldn't see any hope. I didn't want to watch films by myself. I didn't care if I was drinking a first growth claret or a bottle of brake fluid. I didn't care. What's the point? What's the point in pleasure if it isn't a shared pleasure?

So I sat alone each night. But how I longed for him: my lover, my friend, the man with whom I could happily spend the rest of my life and never be bored. I longed for him, and that longing filled my evenings; filled my head as I drove to work; filled my eyes with tears as I looked at my sleeping children each night. It filled my every waking thought. I wanted what other people had. I wanted my old life back. I wanted not to be alone anymore.

> You can deal with the grief, you can vent the anger, you can hide your tears, but you can't do anything about the loneliness.

You might try and cure it by going to evening classes or salsa lessons, but you can't pretend that being with other people is making you forget the one person you long to be with. You can listen to your married friends telling you they would love to have you over for the weekend, and you can even take up their offers, but you know that being with a happily married couple is torture – they might as well have invited you over for a weekend of self-mutilation.

So what is the solution? Well, I can tell you that despite the good intentions of your friends, the cure for loneliness cannot be learned at an evening class. Nor can it be found at the cinema, in a pub or in the bed of a complete stranger. The simple truth of it is that there is no cure. Your loneliness is just one symptom of your grief, and what you are feeling is withdrawal. You are going 'cold turkey'. The person who made you feel happy and alive, who made you feel fulfilled, has been taken away; and your loneliness is just a craving for another fix of their love. In time you grow used to living without the fix. In time you will grow used to spending your evenings alone, but weaning your system off the constant pleasure you received from your lover will be a long, slow process. Don't try to rush it; just understand that it cannot be done in a week, or a month or even a year. The loneliness will be replaced by acceptance – and hopefully, eventually – by another person, but there will be many empty nights, many unfinished meals and hazy recollections of solitary, tearful, drink-sodden outpourings before you can happily spend an evening by yourself.

But you will. Believe me, you will.

~

In summary

- There is no easy cure for loneliness.
- Losing a partner is like being on heroin and being made to go 'cold turkey'; it will take time to wean yourself off the

constant pleasure that your lover gave you.

- Going out into a large social group is likely to make you feel even more alone.
- Weddings are to be avoided at all costs.
- Drinking may fill your lonely evenings, but drinking alone is a very dangerous occupation.
- I know you don't want to hear it, but the only real cure for loneliness is time.

Weekends

It is a cruel paradox that the end of the working week, the time when you are supposed to be at your most relaxed and happy, is the time when you feel most weary and alone. If you have children, the thought of an approaching weekend will fill you with dread; if you don't, then you are looking at two days of enforced solitude.

It is difficult to express just how much I used to loathe the weekend. Nobody could understand why I had developed such an aversion to a time of relaxation and pleasure, but nobody knew just how many painful memories were evoked by the sight of happy fathers with their children. It is impossible to escape happy families at the weekend. There is nowhere you can go and nothing you can do to get away from the stark and painful reality of your single status. It's in your face. Happy mummies with happy daddies; squealing, laughing children playing football, going shopping, enjoying a day out with their doting parents. You start to loathe the very sight of a nuclear family; you'd like to drop a bomb on their smug self-satisfied heads and wipe them off the face of the earth.

And if you don't have children then what do you do? Your friends will almost certainly be reluctant to include you in their plans – after all, nobody wants a sad singleton trailing around, making couples feel awkward and families feel guilty. You are an oddity, a killjoy, a misery who'll cast a weepy shadow on two days of sun. You can't spoil other people's pleasure, so you'd better stay away; stay at home; take your miserable face and turn it to the wall.

> Death marks the end of the happy weekend; death marks the beginning of 48 hours of hell. Death turns Saturday and Sunday into Shattered Day and Shunned Day.

Taking your children out is likely to make them extremely upset, and I have lost count of the times my girls have been reduced to tears by the sight of other children being shown love and affection by their fathers. You will be desperate for a way to entertain your children, but stung by the knowledge that any form of family activity is likely to bring them face to face with reminders of what they have lost. It is impossible to get away from it, so what do you do? Do you stay at home and try to contain the energies of bored youngsters? Do you go out and risk upsetting them? I know, you go and visit friends. That's it. Friends are safe and being with them will make you feel a bit happier. So you plan a weekend away, and at first it's relatively easy because you just have to pack up the car and go. But packing the car and trying to remember everything you need takes thought, and your children will be trying to rush you, taking bags outside and putting them into the boot of the car, ruining your carefully planned system. And you wish there was somebody to help you, because it always used to be so easy, and now it's never easy; it's only ever hard. And then you get cross and the children start to cry and it all seems like too much effort; but you need a break and it'll be fun, so you eventually get the car loaded, start the engine and try to be happy about the trip. The children might be carefree, but you are feeling only stress – stress at the thought of the long drive ahead, of the unbroken silence while the children sleep, and of the effort of trying to keep them entertained and under control when they wake.

And during the weekend you'll try to forget you're alone. People will make a real effort to try and make you feel good, and you will be buoyed up by their enthusiasm and love, and so the weekend passes happily. And then it's time to say goodbye and they stand at the gate and wave you off into the darkening gloom, and you wish with all your heart that you could stay just a little while longer, because the children were so happy and you were relaxed. But you've got to get home.

Normally, you would have dozed off in the car while your partner drove the first leg of the journey, but now you no longer have that luxury. You try to remain alert, but you're tired, the children are gently snoring and you could really do with a snooze yourself. The Sunday roast is sitting in your tummy and the small glass of wine you allowed yourself is having the same effect that lettuce had on the flopsy bunnies. But you can't doze off in the compost heap, you have to drive. So you try to concentrate, but the tiredness and the sadness of being alone make you weep; and all the way back home your eyes are filled with tears and your head is filled with the memories of past journeys in happier times.

And when you get home you have reached such a level of exhaustion and despair that all you want to do is collapse in front of the television with a big glass of wine. But then it begins . . . unpack the car, get the children something for supper, run the bath, unpack all the bags, load the washing machine, get the children into the bath, sort out their clothes for the morning, get them ready for bed, put them to bed, read them a story, make their lunches for the morning . . . And then it's upon you – the weight of the weekend suddenly becomes unbearable and you are overwhelmed by great waves of sadness at the pitiful nature of your solitary existence. So you end the weekend – the relaxing, happy weekend – feeling exhausted and empty, angry and alone.

Sunday, bloody Sunday.

David Robarts wrote this:

> *My absolute worst moment of the week, each and every week bar school holidays, is having to make the sandwiches for the older three's packed lunches on Sunday nights. I don't know why but it's just the straw that breaks this particular camel's back. Is it because it's the last chore of a long weekend of fatherhood and I normally remember just as I've sat down with a drink to vegetate in front of some Sunday night feelgood crap on TV? The other thing I loathe is having to empty the car, unpack suitcases, make the children's tea, bath Felix, put the washing on, empty/fill the dishwasher, feed the dogs and do the homework on top of having just driven back from X, Y or Z. I think Sunday nights should be abolished or moved to a different day of the week.*

I have to confess that I find it difficult to offer any words of advice on how to get through the weekend. It's hard, and that's all there is to it. But what I can say is that once the shock of having to cope all by yourself has subsided, you will begin to work out a system of doing things that will make life a little more bearable for you. It's never going to be easy, but it will certainly stop being intolerable.

My advice for a bearable weekend is as follows:

1. If you have children, try to have a specific outing planned for one of the days.
2. Be prepared for your children to be upset at the sight of other children being shown affection by their father/mother.

3. Be prepared to feel positively miserable at the sight of couples together.

4. Expect to be miserable, and then it'll be a nice surprise if you actually feel a modicum of happiness.

5. If Sunday lunch is too much effort, just take a whole chicken, season and butter its skin, stick half a lemon inside to make it moist and lemony and then put it in the oven with some jacket potatoes. You can make a nice salad, and in a couple of hours you have a simple, delicious and nutritious meal for the whole family.

6. Accept the invitations of friends, but try not to travel too far to visit them, because the long journey home will always be followed by at least two hours of hard work.

7. Try to encourage your children to play at friends' houses, and that way you might get an hour off to read the Sunday papers.

8. Always pour yourself a big drink on Sunday night – you'll need it.

Sandals

Last weekend I decided to take my girls camping. I'm always rather reticent about sleeping under canvas, as it tends to involve a huge amount of effort and a good deal of discomfort. But then I like to think that Rosie and Alice are gaining life skills from sleeping rough, so I invariably give in to their pestering and agree to join the sandal brigade – but for one night and one night only.

I have to confess that I'm an equipment junkie; I don't have any room for Jimmy Choo slingbacks in my closet because most of the space is taken up by scuba equipment. I don't get out much and so prancing around in a wetsuit and BCD in the privacy of my bedroom is about as big a thrill as I get. When I go to a camping shop I have to fight the urge to buy stuff I know I'll never use – but that doesn't stop me wanting it. I try to fight it, but I'm weak – which accounts for the fact that I now own two tents, a fold-up chair, three stoves, lamps, sleeping bags, an electric airbed inflator and a whole heap of paraphernalia that only sees the light of day a couple of times a year.

There is a particular thrill about packing up the car and setting off in search of a perfect pitch. I know it's uncomfortable, and not terribly glamorous, but camping is a really good way to use up an empty weekend. When you're widowed, weekends are about as much fun as amateur dentistry. Nobody wants to be around you, and you don't want to be around anybody else. You are marooned for two endless days, drifting around in a world filled with couples. It's painful at first, but it does become easier over time – which is more than can be said for sleeping on an airbed next to two arm-flailing, teeth-grinding children . . .

The camping went really well, with trips to the beach, fish and chips for supper and bacon and eggs for breakfast. The girls had a great time, but after I'd finished the papers and washed up our plates, I was left with the tricky task of trying not to stick out like a pork chop in a kosher deli. I always feel a bit of a loser when the girls are off playing because I'm left sitting on my own, trying desperately not to look like I'm sitting on my own. I know I should have plucked up the courage to talk to some of the other campers, but just the sight of women with limp, white legs, baggy shorts and drippy husbands is enough to send me scurrying for the safety of my nylon pleasure dome. I can't do it. I'm antisocial – I know it – but there is something faintly odd about people who actually enjoy using a chemical toilet.

I wee on the grass. There, I've said it. When it's dark I really can't be bothered to walk all the way across the campsite to a drafty toilet block. I like to be close to nature. I'm sure that makes me socially unacceptable, but I figure that I couldn't be any more of a social pariah, so go ahead and sue me for grass abuse.

It was a wonderful couple of days, but do you know what? It all went horribly wrong when we got home. I don't mind doing all the work by myself: loading the car, putting up the tent, packing all the stuff away for the journey home, but when I've finished I feel empty and alone. I know I am lucky, and have two lovely girls, but I wish that, just once, I had somebody to say, 'Kate, sit down and have a rest and I'll finish unloading the car. Then I'll put the girls to bed and make us a lovely supper.' I get tired of having to do everything, and all the happiness of the previous two days evaporates in a flood of tears. But it never lasts long. I can't let it. I have to be strong, but sometimes I want to be weak; sometimes I want to be the girl with the pasty complexion and unfortunate choice in sandals, who has a man to bang in the tent pegs and empty the chemical toilet at the end of a blissful weekend. Sometimes, the thought of sitting beside a monosyllabic caravanner is faintly appealing, but then I slap myself and get reality again. I don't need that in my life. Anyway, men with big motorhomes are usually lacking in the trouser department, or so my good friend Sharon tells me, and she should know – she lives in California and they have pretty big motorhomes out there. In fact, I believe in the Sioux language 'Winnebago' means 'stumpy thruster'.

14

the six-month low

I know I have already said that grief will come and go over a long period of time, but in terms of what to prepare for, I feel I have to mention the six-month low. Six months is the time when people will start to leave you to get on with it, because they think that you must be over the worst. But six months is precisely the time when you need them most. It is the moment when the understanding that you are really alone finally hits home – big style.

You may well feel suicidal; you may well feel helpless in the face of what fate has dealt you; you may want to go out and find a totally unsuitable man, or a woman of questionable moral character, just so you don't have to be alone anymore. And if you do choose to get laid by a married man because he's a sure thing and only lives around the corner, or pay a visit to a dodgy massage parlour, then nothing I say will prevent that. What I can say is that at some point around this time you might find yourself reaching the limits of your emotional resources.

In the early weeks your phone will have been ringing off the hook. I spent a good deal of each evening talking on the telephone during that time. People would be desperate to talk to me, to find out how I was and to express their own grief and shock at what had happened. The telephone provided an aural punctuation to the unbroken torture of my mind-locked grief. I would have to speak to people in the midst of tears, and make myself answer when I hadn't spoken to anybody for hours. I soon grew accustomed to being popular; I became voluble and was able to articulate my feelings to those who wanted to hear about my problems. Lots of people rang up to talk to me.

And then they stopped.

Gradually, over time, the calls began to be less frequent, and my evenings became longer. Well, it's only natural that the calls started to peter out – after all, there is only so much sobbing a person can bear to hear before it all becomes a bit tiresome. I didn't blame people for not calling; I just wish they hadn't all decided to do it at the same time. I longed to talk to people, but people had done their bit and now they had left me to get on with it. Six months should be enough time to recover, shouldn't it?

Six months.

And then I felt it hit me. There had been a raft of people and fuss and attention all floating beneath me, keeping me away from the black sea that lay just below. As each person stopped calling, I felt the raft begin to disintegrate. The telephone became silent; this left me with a lot of time to think – and thinking is a dangerous thing for a widow. When you have nothing to distract you, you will start to dwell on all the myriad implications of your enforced solitude. Soon the silence will stop being refreshing and start becoming oppressive, and you will feel yourself being slowly sucked down into the thick, black morass of loneliness.

As a widow, you will find that Father's Day lasts for a fortnight, and that everywhere you go there will be ideas for gifts that you still think about but can no longer buy. And just as the world is peopled by babies for women who are struggling to conceive, so your world is now filled with couples strolling hand in hand, stopping to kiss and touch each other. You will long to be kissed and to be held; you will long to pick his socks up off the floor and iron his shirts. But all you can do is watch and wish your time away.

As a widower, you will long for company, and soon you will find the drudgery of keeping the house clean becoming oppressive and tedious. You will long for soft skin to touch and someone to take care of. You will look at your empty house at the end of each day and wish you were anywhere else but there. If you have children, then the very effort of trying to keep them adequately fed and clothed will be so draining that you will hardly have any energy or thoughts left for yourself.

Looking for answers

It is when you realise that you are actually alone, and might be for some time to come, if not forever, that you will start to be pulled under. Grief will begin to overwhelm you, and your mind will become locked into the task of looking for an answer as to why you have reached such a pitiful state. You will want to find something to help you understand why your partner died. You will be desperate to know if there was anything you could have done that might have prolonged his or her life. You are entitled to see your partner's medical records, and if you ask to see them then your doctor is duty-bound to hand them over to you. And if your husband or wife died in a road accident, then you will want to know if there was any way that it could have been prevented. You will believe that if you can only find an answer to the tragic events that have placed you where you are now, then you might . . . What? You might have been able to make him live a little longer? You might have prevented the tragic chain of events that ended her life? No. It's too late for all that. But that doesn't stop you thinking . . .

Guilt

And along with an unquenchable search for answers you might also become plagued by feelings of guilt. It is irrational and damaging to harbour feelings of guilt about the death of your partner, but that won't stop you feeling them. The guilt may take several forms. You might hate yourself for not giving your husband a hug before he left for work, not knowing that you would never have the chance to hug him again. You might blame yourself for the fact that he worked so hard and ended up dying of a coronary. You might wish that you'd been with your wife in hospital, holding her hand when she died, instead of sleeping at home with your children. You will go back in time and wish that certain things had not happened the way they had; you will try desperately to think of ways that could have made a difference to the final outcome.

Regret

You will also begin to think of all the things you cannot do now. All the plans you made as a couple will come to the forefront of your mind and you will experience a painful longing for everything that has been denied you. Holidays will be particularly significant, as these are a time of togetherness and great joy. They also provoke feelings of intense anticipation and excitement, and therefore the knowledge that you and your partner will never get to swim in the Indian Ocean or visit the Valley of the Kings will become almost too painful to contemplate. I remember saying out loud that I couldn't bear to think that I would never be able to see all of the places that Charlie and I had dreamed of visiting together, and a friend looked at me and said, 'Well, you can visit them on your own.' But I didn't want to see them on my own. I wanted it to be a shared pleasure – just like all of the other shared pleasures that made being married so wonderful.

Eventually, you will become so preoccupied with what you have lost that you will begin to lose the will to go on. When you are tired of searching, when you are tired of wishing, you may think about stopping it all and joining the one you love. I don't believe there is a single widowed person who hasn't contemplated suicide at one time or another. The desire is not prompted purely by depression, but by the desperate need to be with the person for whom life was worth living. The longing to rejoin your dead partner will become so all-consuming that it will start to affect the balance of your already unbalanced mind. Eventually, you will give in totally to the feeling of hopelessness and you will wish that you were dead. You will store up sleeping pills; your mind will wander when you are driving and you will contemplate tweaking the steering wheel just enough to take you into the path of an oncoming lorry or into a brick wall. Now, these are desperate thoughts, irrational thoughts, but normal for anybody who has lost their partner.

With all your heart you will wish for death, but as long as you have children to consider, as long as you have friends and family who care about you, something in your head will tell you that you cannot leave – that you have to stay.

> You have touched bottom. You have gone as low as you can go without actually killing yourself, and when you recognise that you have reached the limits of your endurance, only then will you begin your recovery.

There is no blame to be apportioned, no secret formula that would have prolonged your partner's life, but because you have nobody to blame, you will end up blaming yourself. It is hard to be thankful when life seems so hopeless, but if you try and focus on the happiness that you brought your partner, rather than all the things you didn't do, then you might start to see things differently.

I spent a long time blaming myself for so many things. I tried to piece together all the important events that had helped to shape the outcome of Charlie's life, and then looked at the role I had played. If only I had made Charlie visit the doctor when he began to feel unwell; if only he hadn't been born with a leaking heart valve; if only he hadn't succumbed to such a virulent virus; if only we had been able to enjoy a few more years together; if only Alice could remember her daddy. If only I had been able to tell him just how much I loved him as he lay dying; with my last breath I would have done it. With my last breath I would have whispered my love for him. But I couldn't whisper to him now; all I could do was shout at God with every ounce of my strength for taking that man from me.

It wasn't fair. Life isn't fair, and nor is death.

You can spend the rest of your life trying to find answers; you can spend the rest of your life wishing things had been different. But wishing won't bring your love back. Nothing will bring that person back to you, and the only way you will ever move on is if you can learn to accept what has happened. You must stop wishing and start living.

I no longer blame myself. I believe that all things are meant; that some people are destined to die young and that we must be thankful if we have had the chance to love and be loved, for however short a time.

Forgiving myself took time, and was only possible once I had plumbed the depths of my grief. Watching *Truly, Madly, Deeply* one night while drinking my way through a whole bottle of Rioja certainly helped that process, and I recommend it as the precursor to a really good rant at God for being so unfair. Once you have ranted, shouted and screamed at whosoever you feel like shouting at, then you will feel so much better. Just try not to do it in the supermarket or on the bus, or people might mistake you for some kind of mentalist.

> The recovery process is hard, but coming up out of depression is much easier than going down into it. It is a long, slow process, but once you have made the decision to look to the future, you will find it much easier to accept the past.

In summary

- People will stop calling you after the initial shock has died down.
- Six months is the time when people assume you're over it, but it is exactly the time when you will feel at your lowest ebb.
- Your calendar will start off being filled with appointments and end up as a blank sheet, with nothingness stretching out before you.
- Don't expect to feel like going out – the chances are you will feel so low that you cannot bear to leave the house.
- Six months is the time when the realisation that you are really alone finally hits home.
- Expect to feel extremely low or even suicidal at this point, but don't expect anybody to understand why.
- Understand that when you hit rock bottom, the only way for you to go is up.

15

belongings

what to do with his things

If you can't have him, then you can still have his stuff. You can go to sleep with the shirt that still smells of his aftershave; you can wear his jumper; you can see his toothbrush on your basin and imagine that he will walk in one day, pick it up and use it, just like he always did. And if that's what it takes to make you feel better then so be it. We all need something to help us through our grief, and having something that your partner once wore, used or loved will give you comfort. But it will not bring him back.

> Don't let anybody tell you what to do with his belongings. If you want to throw them all out the day after he is buried, then do it. If you want to keep some of his suits, his razor or his toothbrush, then do it. Nobody can tell you when is the right time to clear out his old jeans and boxer shorts. Nobody.

I kept the turned wooden shaving bowl that Charlie last used on the day he died. I used to look at the swirl of dried lather and imagine the badger bristle shaving brush in his strong hand, curling lazily around the bowl, picking up a soft, pink mound of Trumper's rose shaving soap and rubbing it into his stubbly chin.

I saw that image every time I passed the bowl. I kept the lid on it to preserve the memory. Then one day Rosie found Charlie's shaving brush and ran it around the wooden bowl, just as she'd seen her father do so many times before, destroying the remnants of his final shave; destroying my sacred, tangible memory of him. It was nothing special to her; she didn't know the importance I had placed upon it. I am ashamed of my reaction. When I saw what she'd done I screamed at her and pushed her out of my bedroom.

And all for what?

For a bit of dried lather and nothing more.

Memories are not kept alive in turned wooden bowls; they live on in your heart and in your head. If you keep your bedroom as an untouched and untouchable shrine to your late partner, then how can you ever hope to move on? People are not things. A man is not his suit or his shoes – he may have loved them, but once he is gone they are no longer part of him; they are inanimate objects that grow dusty under the bed and moth-eaten in the wardrobe.

When you can bear to give up the things that were his, then you are starting to let him go. You should let him go.

Give his clothes to a charity shop; make his old shirts into painting overalls for your children – but only when you feel ready to do it. Keep the things that were special to him. Keep his fountain pen, his cufflinks and his favourite suit. Keep his memory alive by talking about him; keep it alive in the minds of his children and, when you are ready, let his things go.

a shrine to the woman you love

You are probably struggling to cope with picking up your socks from the floor, without having to worry about how to tackle your late partner's belongings. You may well have left everything just as it was because you just don't know how to begin to deal with it all. This will give you some comfort for a while at least, but it can be damaging to you in the long term. Most of us would rather put off what we don't want to deal with, and shutting a wardrobe door is easy. If you don't have to look at her clothes then you can forget that they're there. If you leave her dressing table just as it was, then you have a constant reminder of her presence; you can smell her perfume and see her hairs in the hairbrush, and in that way she is still with you.

Of course you should hold on to certain items that were special to your partner, but unless you decide to take up cross-dressing, her skirts and shoes are not going to be a lot of use to you. If you have daughters then you should try to get them involved before you discard anything. It will take a great deal of tact and strength to explain to your children that you want to dispose of most of their mother's belongings, particularly if you choose to do it early on, but if you include them and explain why you are doing it, I'm sure they will understand. Handbags and shoes are always useful for the dressing-up box, and if you have teenage daughters I'm sure they will want to save certain items for themselves. My children know why I have disposed of most of Charlie's clothes, and as I write there is a bag of shoes I have just found at the back of the wardrobe, waiting to go to the local charity shop. My girls don't have any emotional attachment to Charlie's old clothes because they know that I don't. I still have a few special items of clothing in the wardrobe that are too precious to give away, but everything else has gone.

There is no need to rush in to anything – it may take months or even years before you can bring yourself to take your late partner's clothes to the charity shop, but you will feel so much better when you do. If you cannot bring yourself to sort out your partner's personal effects, ask a female friend to help you. It will be difficult for you both, but holding on to your partner's possessions because you can't bear to be without her will only prolong your grief.

As I have said, nobody can tell you when it is the right time to get rid of your partner's personal belongings, but what you must understand is that you cannot hope to move forward if you are still dwelling in the past. You will know when the time is right, and if you do decide to heave the whole lot into the Salvation Army collection bin on the day after the funeral, then that is what you must do.

Bolts

This week, a nice couple from Tiverton are coming to buy our climbing frame. Assembling it was one of the last things Charlie and I ever did together. You might therefore assume that I wouldn't want to get rid of it because of all the associated memories, but to me it's just a big collection of metal bars, lying on the barn floor awaiting collection.

I have no sentimental attachment to the climbing frame, but the memory of the day we got it is firmly stored away. It was a blustery spring day and there was a slight drizzle, which made handling the large metal posts and tiny nuts quite awkward, but we worked at it together, and in a couple of hours it was up. It was a long, fiddly job, but the morning passed without a single cross word. When it was finished,

Charlie sat and rested with Rosie and I came out with a pot of tea and some homemade ginger cake; and then we all watched in horror as a giggling Alice fell from the top platform of her new plaything and bounced onto the grass below. Luckily she was unhurt, and so we gave her a cuddle, fed her some cake and sat and admired the fruits of our labours. I have a picture of my girls on the glider swing soon afterwards, laughing in the sunshine of an Easter weekend. Charlie isn't in the photograph because he'd died a week earlier, but my girls were happily swinging; swinging and laughing in the warm spring sun.

The climbing frame brings back lots of memories, and now it's in bits, but I am not. I will not hold on to things just because they have an association with Charlie, and for my girls, seeing that I'm not upset about letting things go helps them to understand that life has moved forward, and that I have too. They are happy to see the climbing frame go; Rosie helped me to take it apart, just as her daddy had helped me to put it together, and there was a beautiful symmetry in that for me. And if I needed any further evidence that my girls have accepted the loss of their father, I got it yesterday when they asked if we could make a collage of photographs. I assumed it would include pictures of Charlie, but Rosie said, 'No, Mummy, I want it to be just the three of us – our family as it is now.' She is only 10 years old, but somehow her understanding of life and loss goes way beyond her years, and I am grateful for that, and for the fact that we are a happy family, despite everything we've had to endure.

Yesterday we went for a walk to Blackdown rings. The rings are the remains of an Iron Age settlement perched on a hill near our village. They have stunning views, and at this time of year swathes of bluebells carpet the ditches and battlements. The air was heady with the rich coconut scent of gorse flowers, and filled our lungs as we raced and tumbled through the glistening bluebells. We chased sheep, chased each other and laughed until we were hoarse; and as we stood to catch our breath and looked out across the patchwork of fields to the sea beyond, I thought how wonderful it was that I have two little girls who are so happy and so resolute. They know their daddy is with them, in their hearts and in their heads; he's not in a metal ladder or on a swing; he's not tied to a jumble of bars and bolts; he's part of them and part of me, and he always will be.

And when the nice man comes to take away the climbing frame, he'll never know that Charlie was the man who built it; he'll take it home and his two little boys will be able to laugh and swing in the warm spring sunshine. And that climbing frame will begin to take on a whole new host of associated memories, which is just as it should be, because things do not hold the memories of people; people do.

16

birthdays and other significant days

The grieving process is a long and difficult journey, and standing out like hurdles on the path to normality are all the significant events you used to celebrate, but which you now want only to forget. But there is no getting away from them. There are only so many wedding invitations you can refuse, only so many card shops you can avert your eyes from in the week before Mother's Day, only so much 'Bah, humbug' you can mutter at Christmas. At some stage you will have to face these obstacles, and sooner or later one of them will bring you crashing to the floor.

weddings

Weddings are especially difficult and should be avoided in the first year if at all possible. Family weddings cannot be avoided, and so you should try and prepare yourself for what is to come. It will be an occasion of great joy for the happy couple, but you may find it hard to share their joy, however much you love them. You will try, for their sake, to smile for the wedding photographer, but all the while you will be longing to walk away. Seeing two people setting out on a journey, which for you has just ended, will be extremely difficult. You will be reminded of your own wedding, and that memory will fill you with untold sadness – sadness you will have to disguise when all about you are happy faces. The sight of so many people celebrating what you have just lost will reduce you to tears, but you will not want to be seen to be crying, just in case your distress spoils the happy day for other people. And so you will be brave, for the sake of your family; you will get through the day as best you can and you will leave feeling empty and alone.

birthdays

Birthdays are also difficult. You may well wander around the shops, musing on what to buy for your partner's birthday, before you realise that dead people don't have birthdays. Your own birthday will be even more difficult. If you don't have any children, then it will be a very lonely, empty day. You should try to buy yourself a small treat, just so you have something nice to open. Your friends and family will be especially aware of how you are feeling, and will almost certainly try to make you feel special in some way, either by taking you out or by giving you a present. In any event, you should try to remember that it is only a day, a day like any other, and that building it up into something important will only cause you pain. You will have to employ all your skills of tact and diplomacy when you are given your birthday gifts, because brevity and bluntness will have replaced the standard methods of trying to disguise disappointment at being given yet another foot spa or hideous pair of slippers. Death makes us brutally honest. It removes artifice. It makes people see us as raw, vulnerable human beings. Raw, vulnerable human beings who do not want toasters or patterned jumpers, but who just don't have the strength or the will to say so. All we want is what we cannot have – our love back.

If you have children, then birthdays will be difficult for other reasons. My oldest daughter did not get especially upset when it was her own birthday, but when it came to other children's birthdays it was a different matter. Rosie would invariably end up in tears at the end of each birthday party; I got quite used to concerned parents telling me that she had spent almost the entire party in floods of tears. Rosie wanted to have a good time, but as soon as she realised she was enjoying herself, she felt guilty. She thought that it was an act of disloyalty to her daddy if she laughed, and so as soon as she found herself laughing, she would become upset, and the laughter would turn to tears. It took a couple of years before she felt confident enough to go to a party without feeling that she was going to spoil it for everybody by getting upset. Thankfully she now understands that laughter at a birthday party is not an act of betrayal, and is just as happy as every other child.

christmas

Christmas is unavoidable. Your first Christmas alone will be hellish, and it would be best spent among friends or family. But even in the midst of loving family you are likely to feel very uncomfortable. For a woman it is all to do with the giving of presents. Sitting and watching couples exchanging gifts will only remind you of all the things you would like to have bought for your husband. It will remind you of all the lovely things he bought for you in the past, and of the love that went into choosing them. And if he never bought you anything nice, then you will be thinking of all the useless kitchen gadgets and unfortunate red, lacy knickers that are now all you have to remind you of his presents – and his presence – at Christmas.

For a man, Christmas is difficult for a number of reasons. If you have children, you may well be faced with organising the whole thing for the first time ever. You might have left the buying of presents to your partner, which is what a lot of men tend to do because of a rabid aversion to shopping. Consequently, trying to coordinate the Herculean task of organising Christmas, while trying to hold down a job and/or look after the children may well prove virtually impossible. Men often leave everything to their partners, or to the last minute, or both.

If you cannot face the prospect of Christmas, just take a step back and think about what really needs to be done and what can be put off. You don't have to go out into the thronging crowds and battle with other weary shoppers to get what you want. The Internet is a great place to buy presents, and if you plan far enough in advance you can get all the toys and games your children need with the minimum amount of fuss. It is also a great place for finding presents for teenagers – I saved £50 on the price of an MP3 player last year, and got all of my CDs and DVDs in November to save myself the trouble of trudging through the shops. You can forget about writing Christmas cards – people will understand – and don't worry about Christmas lunch if you can't cook or don't have the heart to try – either take the family out for lunch or try to get yourself an invitation to someone else's house. I would find it hard to imagine that there isn't somebody who would take pity on a poor, lonely widower and look after him on Christmas day.

If you are alone at Christmas you could just forget all about it: don't decorate, don't send any cards, don't do anything that means you have to celebrate an event which only brings back painful memories and makes you deeply unhappy. There is no law against ignoring Christmas; you might want to get something special to eat on Christmas Day, but forcing yourself to be happy and sociable for the sake of others is never a good idea. If you do feel like accepting invitations to go out alone during the festive season, then you must also be prepared for a whole host of questions and comments like, 'Are you doing anything special on Christmas Day?' or 'It must be so hard for you at this time of year.' People will be feeling all happy and festive while trying their hardest to avoid saying anything that might upset you, and this can lead to some excruciatingly embarrassing incidents.

My all-time winner came at a drinks party, which I attended only a few weeks after Charlie's death. Most of the people at the party whom I knew hadn't seen me since the funeral, and one particular friend came bounding up to me and said, 'Hi, Kate, how are yoo . . . o . . . o?' I saw a look of realisation flash across his face as he remembered what had actually happened since we last met, and this sudden recall effected temporary facial paralysis. He stood, mid-sentence, with his mouth open, and a fixed grin on his face, totally unable to utter another word. He stood like that for several seconds before I opted to change the subject and released him from suspended animation. There was only one place to go after that, and that was home.

> There will come a time when you can enjoy Christmas again, but attendance is not compulsory, so if you don't feel like it, just stay away.

If you have children, then Christmas is something you will have to grin and bear. The children will be expecting the same amount of excitement and the same number of presents as usual. You may not be in a position to be able to afford to give them everything they want, so only buy what you can easily afford and try to remind them that things are different for you now. Anyway, other people are bound to spoil them, so you really shouldn't worry. Being with other people at Christmas will help greatly, and if there are other children to play with then you might be able to grab a few moments of quiet reflection.

I spent the first few Christmas holidays after Charlie's death with his family, but I can't pretend that I found it easy. Being in a strange bed on Christmas morning just isn't the same; and it has to be said that there is something rather wonderful about slobbing about in pyjamas until midday and doing nothing in particular. My girls and I now stay at home for Christmas, and we all seem to prefer it that way.

As a rule, just do what you think is best for you and your children, and don't feel under pressure either to visit relatives or to invite them over to your house. We all know that Christmas brings out the worst in family tensions, and you cannot afford to get upset over Trivial Pursuit or who is in charge of the remote control when your whole world has just crumbled about your ears. Expect the worst at Christmas, especially in the first couple of years, and try to focus on what comes after it. Just fix a smile on your face and get through it any way you can. The laughter of children is the best tonic you can have at this time, so try to make the most of it.

new year

New Year's Eve sucks the big one. I never really liked it when Charlie was alive, but my God, how I hate it now. It is built up to be this big, happy event when people get together and have a fantastic time, but in reality I think it nearly always ends up as one great big letdown. There is a false sense of importance attached to it, and you should not attach any importance to it whatsoever. People get all hyped up over what is essentially a great excuse to stay at home and watch Jools Holland, and if there is one event guaranteed to make you feel even more miserable and alone than you already do, then New Year's Eve is it.

I spent one memorable New Year's Eve trying to conjure Charlie out of the ether. The room was candlelit; I'd had a nice meal courtesy of my friends Walker and Deb, followed by a significant quantity of Madeira and had smoked a big, fat Monte Cristo cigar. (I smoke one each New Year's Eve for Charlie. He gave up smoking on the day he met me but I'd promised him he could have a cigar on New Year's Eve 1999. He never got to smoke his cigar, and so each New Year's Eve, just before midnight, I sit on the flat roof overlooking the village square and have one for him. I blow the smoke heavenwards, and as it drifts up into the starry night sky I like to imagine him leaning over a cloud, inhaling deeply.)

Anyway, I was nicely relaxed and thought it would be a good time to receive a visitation from my beloved. I think it may have been the George Michael track that was playing that he didn't like, because he wouldn't appear for me, no matter how hard I willed him to. I've stopped trying to see Charlie on New Year's Eve. I know he's around and I think it would scare the bejesus out of me if he suddenly appeared at the foot of my bed. My recipe for a perfect New Year's Eve in the early years of bereavement is a nice meal, followed by a mug of Horlicks and an early night. If you do want to go out, get drunk and then stand alone while other couples snog on the stroke of midnight, then go right ahead – but don't say I didn't warn you. You will invariably wake up the next morning with a thumping hangover and a feeling of deep disillusionment – and if that is how you want to greet the New Year then so be it.

anniversary of the death

The anniversary of your partner's death will undoubtedly be one of the most significant hurdles you will have to face. It may send you spiralling into depression, but if you are like me, you will see it as a milestone on the road to your recovery. Strangely, I did not feel sad – I felt elated. I knew I had triumphed on that day, and I honestly believed I could face anything that fate had to throw at me once it was over. I am not suggesting that you will feel the same way, but I do hope you will feel a certain sense of achieve-ment at surviving the trials of the previous year.

You will probably receive many cards and bouquets of flowers, and it is likely that many will come from people whom you haven't heard from in a while. If you are not feeling depressed or especially sad, then others might think it strange, but others have not been feeling what you have been feeling for the last 12 months. You will have thought of your partner every day to a varying degree, and you will think about them to varying degrees every day for the rest of your life. Other people forget – it is human nature to do so – but they will remember on that particular day and will want to let you know they are thinking of you. It is always nice to receive flowers, and getting cards from people you haven't heard from in a while will give you an excuse to get back in touch with them.

The anniversary might well have an unexpected effect on your child. I thought my daughter Rosie was over the worst of her grief when I took her down to Charlie's grave on the second anniversary of his death, but I was totally unprepared for the reaction that followed. Visiting the grave on that day triggered an extreme reaction, culminating with my five-year-old daughter telling me she wanted to die so that she could be with her daddy again. It is heartbreaking for any parent to hear their own child expressing the wish to die, but sometimes we all need a shock like that to make us realise what that child is really feeling.

Robin Walker experienced similar problems:

Around this time there were a lot of situation-specific memories brought on for me by the start of autumn and the reminders of September 11th, the anniversary of my wife's death. During this time I lost a lot of weight and felt closer to a complete emotional collapse than at any stage since Zoe's death. My son Alex also went through a change in behaviour and may have had situation-specific memories. He had also started at a new nursery school (part-time at first) and was therefore seeing less of his nanny. He became difficult, demanding, woke up often during the night, and was almost aggressive at times. He may not, however, have behaved very much differently to other three-year-olds undergoing a big change (such as a new school or arrival of a sibling), and I have always cautioned against assuming his behaviour is much different from that of other, similar-aged children. This difficult period went on for months, and what helped was me going away for a week's holiday without Alex. He stayed with his grandparents. After the break he was much better and settled into his nursery school. Things have been much better since.

Grief does not have a specific timescale, especially in the case of a child, so you must be prepared for an extreme reaction on a day of particular significance, and you should try to deal with it accordingly.

Weddings, anniversaries and birthdays are not always happy days for you or your children and you must spend them in ways that are going to cause you least distress. In time they will become easier and a great deal more enjoyable, but don't feel you have to enjoy them just because other people expect you to. Do what you feel is right and always remember that it is only one day out of your life. Cross it off your calendar when it is over and then move on.

~

In summary

- Significant anniversaries will almost certainly send you spiralling into depression.
- Christmas is a hellish time for all widowed people. Friends and family will expect you to be happy, and you'll feel like sticking your head in the oven alongside the turkey.
- If you are alone, consider spending Christmas at a hotel with a singles group, but don't feel you have to celebrate an event that makes you miserable.
- Try and do your Christmas shopping on-line.
- Your child may find it very difficult at school before Father's or Mother's Day, because most schools encourage children to make cards. If your child is too upset to make a card then you should make his or her teacher aware of this. I have heard of a little boy being told that he wasn't able to make a Father's Day card because he didn't have a father. If any teacher has the temerity to suggest that your child cannot make a card for

a dead parent then go straight to the headteacher and make a formal complaint.

- ■ It is vitally important that your child can express his or her love at any time for a parent who has died, and making a card and taking it down to the graveside is never a bad thing.
- ■ Your own birthday will be a horribly depressing day.
- ■ New Year's Eve sucks.
- ■ As a general rule, the times when other people celebrate and are happiest are the times when you will feel the most miserable.

Wonwell

It's my wedding anniversary today, and although I remembered last week, today it completely slipped my mind. I remained completely oblivious until my mother-in-law phoned to see how I was. I was pretty chipper actually, and so I think my chirpy tone took her a bit by surprise; but I'm not going to get all weepy and maudlin just because it's the anniversary of something that no longer exists. You may think me callous and unfeeling, especially if you're recently widowed, but by letting you know how I feel today, I hope you will understand that it's alright to forget a wedding anniversary, and that there shouldn't be a burden upon you to constantly remind yourself of what you have lost, but simply to enjoy your life as it is now.

Charlie is no longer my husband and so our wedding anniversary is no longer a significant event in my life. In the early days I used to get upset every time 20 May came around because I remembered what a joyous day it always was in our lives. It was a day when Charlie would buy me a special gift, or cook me a delicious meal, and when I would reflect upon just how lucky I was to be married to him. Such an occasion deserved to be remembered, but now it's just another day in

---

May. I can't feel sad on such a gorgeous day; I want to be happy because my garden is looking beautiful, my goldfish are healthy and my vegetables are bursting out of the ground.

Rosie and Alice came home from school this afternoon and begged me to take them to the beach. They don't know it's my wedding anniversary; all they know is that it's hot and they want to paddle in the sea. We decided to go to our nearest beach, which lies at the end of a tiny country lane; it's perilously narrow and designed only for the brave – caravans, lorries and old people who cannot reverse are not allowed to travel down its leafy loveliness, which is the best recommendation I know to go there.

The Devon lanes are at their most beautiful at the moment – high, green banks thronged with red campion, bluebells and wild garlic – and as we drove along and brushed past the flowers we released a fragrance redolent of taking a stroll through Gérard Depardieu's whiskers. The trees that topped the banks formed a verdant archway through which we passed, weaving up and down the sun-dappled lane until we got to our destination.

We spent a happy hour by the water's edge, laughing and skimming stones. Alice ran up and down like a child of nature and Rosie sat by my side and sipped Lapsang Suchong. She likes to be close to me; she's my chum and I love her with all my heart. And little Alice; well, she ran straight up to me, buried her head in my chest and hugged me with all her might. It was just my two girls and me, on a sunny afternoon in May – a moment in time that is really worth remembering.

You cannot feel sad on such a day. Life is worth living at times like this; sunshine and happiness flow through me and memories of mourning and misery are left far behind.

And if you're reading this and thinking that I'm a smug cow who has no idea how you feel – I do. I know what it's like to live in a world of darkness; I know what it's like to associate all the good things in life with someone who can no longer enjoy them; I know what it's like to live a tainted life. But the misery does not last, and eventually joy and light flood back into your life. You learn to enjoy things for their own sake, and stop resenting feeling pleasure because of its association with the past.

I want to give a message of hope to all those hopeless people who are reading my words. I want to shout from the rooftops that life can be good again. And I want to drive to Wonwell beach again on a sunny afternoon in May, because driving down that lane was a true taste of heaven. I felt that Charlie was smiling down on our little car as we brushed past the bright, white garlic and swept under the vibrant green branches of the overhanging trees. Today was a joyous day – 20 May, anniversary of teaching my girls to skim stones.

17

sink or swim

When is it going to get better? Isn't it supposed to get better, to get easier? Isn't the sadness supposed to fade? Isn't the pain supposed to ease? They don't give you a timetable, those sombre funeral directors; you don't get a standing order from the bank, which pays off your grief each month, leaving you free of sorrow at the end of the year. So how long does it take? Well, that all depends on you. I have met women with dead, emotionless eyes who are clearly still deeply depressed 20 years after the death of their husbands. I could not imagine crying about Charlie's death after that length of time, but those women were still in tears.

I have cried though. I have wept and wailed and sobbed myself to sleep on more occasions than I care to mention. I have screamed and shouted and cried until I was too exhausted to produce any more tears. But if I were still crying now I would worry. I don't feel the need to cry about Charlie because I have long since opened up the floodgates and released my grief over his death. If I got tearful when speaking about him, six years after his death, then I would know that my grief had not been resolved, and that there were still issues I had to face up to.

I have never felt any anger towards Charlie for leaving me; I could never feel any ill will towards a man who had no control over his fate. People do not choose to die. Men do not harbour a secret wish to be eaten away by cancer, and women do not pray to be struck by a passing car so that they can leave their children without a mother. Any anger we feel should be vented, but hating your partner for something they had no control over seems futile to me. It is a negative exercise, and if you become accustomed to viewing your situation entirely negatively, then it will be very difficult for you to find any kind of happiness in the future.

I realised early on that my ability to survive what had happened was entirely dependent on the way I viewed my current situation. If I saw myself as a victim, as a helpless individual who was powerless to change the God-awful hand fate had dealt out, then I may as well have called myself a punch-bag and walked along the street inviting people to take a swing at me. Yes, death sucks; yes, life is hard when you are on your own and you know there is nobody out there who is thinking about you. Yes, it is a sad and lonely job bringing up children on your own, or wishing you had been able to have a child before your partner died – but we have to try to get past all of that. It all takes time, but just how long it takes is up to you.

I knew it was up to me whether or not I gave in to the hopelessness of my situation and spent the rest of my life as a depressed individual who was unable to find joy in any aspect of life. It was up to me whether or not I decided to drag myself up by my bootstraps and make a new life for myself. I had to decide.

But as I write this, I know there are many people out there who did not have the marriage I had. I know there are many people whose self-esteem was so low before the death of their partner that they see no possible hope of finding future happiness. I understand that my life has been blessed and not blighted, but I also believe that we are all possessed of the ability to heal ourselves. Something in you will have died when you lost your partner, but so much remains alive. The potential for happiness lies within you; the potential to make another person happy lies within you; but if you don't have the will or the inclination to recognise that life can be good again, then what hope is there?

You have to try and see past what afflicts you now and look to your future. Make yourself believe you will be happy again; make yourself change the way you look, the way the house looks, the way you live your life. Nobody is going to do it for you – it is you who must instigate the change. Everyone needs to feel safe and secure, but sometimes clinging on to what made us happy in a past life will stop us making a new life for ourselves.

The mind has an infinite ability to heal the deepest emotional wounds, but it has to be given a chance to do so. Reaching for a bottle of Prozac when you feel you can't cope any more will provide short-term relief, but may lead to long-term dependency. Drinking a bottle of wine a day may help to dull the pain and get you to sleep at night, but pouring alcohol into an open wound will only serve to keep it as red and as raw as the day it was made. Turning away from the problem will only serve to bring you face to face with a bigger problem somewhere down the line, so you must stop believing that you are a helpless victim and start to believe in your ability to overcome death. You cannot expect things to change overnight, but finding one positive aspect to your situation will be a start.

If you feel you don't have the strength to go through the reasoning process alone, you should try and find someone who can act as your guide. If you have spent your whole life being told what to do by others, it will not be easy to think for yourself. If you grew up with an overbearing mother who made you feel worthless and insecure, then you are not suddenly going to be able to find the strength to work through your grief simply because I am telling you that you can. There are many good counsellors who are almost certain to be able to provide you with the help you need, but equally you might find yourself in the hands of a person who has absolutely no idea of how to help you, and that may set your recovery back a long way. For more about counselling, see page 93.

> Don't expect to wake up one morning with a beaming smile on your face and a big, bouncy spring in your step. You have to give yourself time and you have to let your mind become clear enough to allow you to work through all that has happened, and make some sense of it.

A mind dulled by drugs or alcohol will never allow you sufficient insight into your plight and will not be able to provide you with any kind of resolution. Your mind must be sharp and open to cognitive thought. This will not be possible for some time after the death of your partner, and the exact time will vary considerably, depending on your circumstances. The important thing is to be open to change, and once you can find a single reason for joy in life, then you will begin to find others. Learning to adapt to a new way of living is the key: your life has changed and trying to hang on to your old life will only hold you back.

I started off thinking how tragic it was that my beloved husband should be taken away from his family at such a young age. I raged against the injustice of such a kind and loving individual having to suffer long and painful treatments, when all around me there seemed to be hateful, evil individuals who breezed through life without even so much as a broken nail. Life seemed so terribly unfair. But gradually my feelings of hate and regret turned into acceptance and optimism. Because I didn't let anybody else think for me – and because I didn't try to block out the process of reasoning which is so vital to recovery – my mind was able to work through all the things I saw as negative and come to a rational understanding, and eventually a positive outlook. I began to accept that Charlie's kindness and generosity of spirit, his love of others and his unconditional love for his family were borne out of the knowledge that his life might be cut short at any moment. I began to understand that the strength of my love for him was borne of the same knowledge, and that I was driven by the need to live every second of my life with him to the fullest extent, to joy in him and to make him the happiest man on earth. Yes, he suffered. Yes, he was taken from me, taken from his daughters, his family and all those who loved him. Yes, he died too young, but what he gave during his short life was a rare and precious thing, and something to be treasured, not squandered on bitterness and regret.

A man wrote to me recently to say that he had not smiled since the death of his wife, and that he thought he would never smile again. I asked him if he thought that was what his wife would have wanted. I asked him if he was going to drop his head and let himself be beaten, or whether he was going to stand up and face all those people who had written him off as a hopeless case and say, 'Fuck you. I can do this. I can stand up and take this, just watch me.'

We could all drop our heads; we could all say, 'I'm never going to smile again because I have nothing to be happy about.' We could all give up because life feels hopeless, but some of us choose not to. Some of us poor, bewildered souls find that acceptance is better than bitterness; that thankfulness is better than regret. Some of us decide to swim against the tide of fate, and others sink slowly below the surface into the dark, hushed world of despondency, never to be seen again.

I have so much to be thankful for. I refuse to live the rest of my life thinking that I'm unlucky. I walk down the street, the blackness of my mourning now a suit of gilded armour, my resolve and self-belief, my sword and shield.

Nothing can touch me now.

Sink or swim, victim or vanquisher – the choice is yours.

Growth

Today I'd like to pay tribute to the two people who vet the content of my on-line journal. They've never met me and they've never met each other, but I trust them implicitly, and one of these days I'm going to take them both out and get them horribly drunk.

David Robarts and Sarah Snaydon come from wildly differing backgrounds, have divergent political beliefs, and live hundreds of miles away from each other and from me. Our commonality lies in the fact that we're all sad bastards without partners.

Sarah first wrote to me in November 2002. Her husband Geoff had died on the day the merrywidow website was born, and she'd typed a short, unsentimental note to thank me for what I'd written. The note was unremarkable and the language plain, but what made me sit up and take notice was that it was typed in red. Her e-mail contained not a trace of self-pity, but her true emotions bled from the screen. I was witness to the exsanguination of a widow. She'd lost her husband, her lover, her life-blood, and she was trying to hold herself together in order to thank me. She had no need to thank me.

David wrote to me shortly afterwards. His e-mail was dark and expansive, bleak and unremitting. The ferocity of the medical facts that bombarded me made me weep, and I found it hard to imagine how any man could hold himself together under such horrific circumstances. David could only stand helplessly by and watch as his wife's flesh was greedily consumed by the ravages of meningococcal septicaemia. Titania died slowly, died by inches; lost both legs and eventually lost the will to go on. She was a remarkably courageous woman who left behind four young children and a broken-hearted man.

Life seemed hopeless for David and Sarah in the winter of 2002, and I really worried about the chances of either of them ever regaining any sense of optimism about the future. David's life was a nightmare juggling act of baby feeding, school runs and supper detail. Sarah had two teenage daughters to bring up single-handed, and a teaching job to hold down. Most people who write to me for help will only write once; some people write to thank me for replying so promptly, but generally two e-mails are about all I get. Sarah and David kept writing, and through their e-mails I was able to gauge their state of mind. I wanted to carry them both in the early days. I wanted to wrap them both up in my arms and make all the hurt and the pain disappear, but all I could do was keep on writing and hope that they would find the strength to carry on.

The question I get asked most often is, 'When am I going to start feeling better?' I try to explain that grief is a journey, a long and difficult journey to self-belief and acceptance. David and Sarah were walking along a road and all they could see in the distance was a sign saying 'Dead End'. But I could see further. I couldn't make their journey any easier, but I knew I could walk beside them, offering encouragement and understanding. I knew they would be fine, because they each possessed two vital assets: a sense of humour and a positive outlook.

Watching other people come though the grieving process is like teaching a young child to ride a bike without stabilisers. When you lose your partner it is almost impossible to maintain any kind of mental or emotional balance. You lurch from depression to mania but lack the necessary mental strength to gain forward momentum. In the first year David and Sarah frequently wobbled, but somehow managed to remain upright. Sarah took her first holiday as a single mother and sent me a photograph when she returned home. She'd hooked up with a couple of delightful gay men; unthreatening, supportive holiday companions who gave her the opportunity to laugh for the first time in months. David gradually took to the role of single parent, and allowed each of his four children the chance to fully express their grief. They helped him design Titania's headstone, and now they are helping him to rebuild his life.

Sarah's daughters are still struggling to come to terms with the loss of their father, and I know that Sarah freely admits that she still cannot describe herself as truly happy. But she's making remarkable progress and has just returned to the field of amateur dramatics, which I know is something she thought she'd never do. She no longer writes in terse, red sentences, but instead chooses to write hysterically funny, wonderfully expansive e-mails, which tell the story of a woman who is rediscovering her self-confidence and her voice.

David is now strong enough to be able to offer emotional support to others, and is feeling happy and confident about the future. His e-mails are funny, eloquent and as singular as the malt he's no doubt enjoying at this very moment. He can be quite a stern critic, but I value his judgement because he's got a much bigger brain than me.

Two people, seemingly unconnected but joined by a mutual burden of grief, have walked along a road less travelled. I did nothing more than watch over them as they journeyed on through the darkness and out into the light; but I watched with pride, and I hope that I never lose sight of David Robarts and Sarah Snaydon.

part two
out into the light

18

the social whirl

By now you must be getting lots of invitations to go out.

No?

Are married couples who used to ask you to dinner or down to the pub trying to avoid you?

Well, as a widow or widower, you have to realise what you are now: a relatively normal, single person, in the same age group as all your married friends – but with latent, and possibly very powerful, unfulfilled sexual needs. You are a dangerous guest to casually toss among couples who have been married for maybe a decade and who are possibly slightly bored with their own sex lives. You may not see yourself as a threat, unless you really want to ruin the marriage of a trusted friend, but your friends might see you as a bit of a loose cannon, and prefer to keep you at arm's length. If you do get invited out to meet a selection of eligible, single people, then good luck to you, but there is every chance that you will not.

In India, Brahman society dictates that a young widow is

made 'socially dead'; to this end she must undergo tonsure, which means that her head is ritually shaved. A woman's hair is seen in many societies as a symbol of her sexuality, and shaving the head of a young Brahman widow gives others control over that sexuality. The dichotomy of this belief is that while others see young widows as sexually threatening, we see ourselves as temporarily neutered. Any woman who really loved her husband does not suddenly start looking for another mate as soon as he's shuffled off this mortal coil. We just don't do it. You can't suddenly flick a switch and divert years of love and desire to another man. That is why women take so long to remarry; we may be sexually active and desirous of sexual gratification, but we wouldn't dream of seeking it from a new man until we have come to terms with the loss of our husband. Widows are not heat-seeking missiles that lock onto other women's partners the moment they enter the same air space. I, for one, apply the same rigorous moral code that I had before I was married to Charlie, and that means that all married men are out of bounds. But try telling that to a nervous wife – they don't believe it, and I'm sure most of them would be more than happy to break out the hair clippers given half a chance.

Head shaving is an extreme example of social exclusion, but in Britain we have some really imaginative ways of kicking a woman when she's down. I heard from one widow who told me that she used to have a great social life when her husband was alive. They regularly entertained, and therefore after his death she rightly expected her friends to rally round and invite her to dinner. And what happened? Can you guess? Has it happened to you? Well it's happened to me and it's not funny at all. Where do they go, those people who used to visit with monotonous regularity, eat your food, drink your wine and then walk out into the night saying, 'We must have you over soon?' Well, I can tell you if you don't already know. They carry on just as before, only they cross you off their 'must have over' list, and put you on the reject pile. There you sit with flatulent men and braying women; there you sit with the vicar and the cleaning lady. You can forget invitations to supper because you don't exist socially any more. People will still talk to you in the street, and when they bump into you inadvertently, they will always say, 'I was meaning to give you a ring to see how you were doing.' But they won't ring you up and ask you to dinner.

Widowers can also find it difficult to re-enter the social scene. They may not encounter the same problems as their female counterparts, but it can still be hard, as Richard Martin explains:

Getting back into the social scene is not easy. While my male friends do not view me as a threat to their marriages, none-theless, as a single man among many couples, the nature of the invitations has changed. With one or two exceptions, gone are the dinner party invitations. These have been replaced by suppers with individual couples and buffet parties with 12 or 15 other friends. I clearly present an awkward challenge.

On the other side of the coin, I have made an effort to continue inviting friends here. I've had a couple of dinners, a buffet supper and a get-together for drinks at Christmas. Hard though this is, I felt it was important to 'keep in the loop'. However, my limited culinary skills have been tested and have had to be supplemented with help from my daughter and M&S – another challenge for the male!

There is a fundamental difference in the way men and women are treated when they become widowed. For a simple explanation, just take a look in any junior school playground. Boys play rough games. There's always a lot of pushing and shouting but, generally speaking, most boys tend to get on together, and fisticuffs or the exchange of marbles quickly resolve any disputes. Girls are a different proposition altogether; they form cliques, and if a dispute arises, the protagonists do battle with catty words, dirty looks and the worst punishment of all – social exclusion. Being excluded from a group of girls that you long to be a part of can be devastating . . . Fast-forward 30 years or so and not much has changed – married men are not usually compromised by the presence of a lone male, and therefore tend to be very accepting; but women seem to find it much harder to accept the inclusion of a lone female into their social circle.

The woman I mentioned earlier was surprised when the dinner invitations dried up, but a bigger shock was to come. One couple, who obviously felt a little guilty about excluding their poor widowed friend, decided to drive round to her house on the night of each social gathering from which she had been excluded, bringing with them a selection from the menu for her to eat on her own. Imagine her joy at being given a doggie bag as a consolation prize. Staggering, but true.

So what can you do? Well, the answer is that you can't do anything. You can't do anything about losing your partner – the person who was not just your lover and your best friend, but your key to respectability. All you can do is turn the situation around and invite people who have been kind to you to supper – you don't have to cook anything spectacular; the plain fact of it is that you can thank people by making an effort for them. When you feel there is no way you can repay a great kindness, you can – by cooking.

My friends come to supper regularly. I did go through a stage of having dinner parties, but keeping people entertained and single-handedly doing all the cooking is such a huge effort that I tend to keep it small and simple now. One of my friends who comes over regularly always says, 'You can taste the love in this food.' And she's right. I show love for my friends by cooking for them – simple, but effective.

coping with social exclusion

Social exclusion can be hurtful and damaging, but for it to happen when you are at your weakest and most vulnerable is something that can be hard to bear. And what does this tell you about those people who used to call themselves your friends? Well, you don't have to be a rocket scientist to see that all those who enjoyed your hospitality and yet deny you theirs are not the friends you thought they were. It is one of the lessons of widowhood, and is not easy to accept.

> People will desert you at a time when you need them most. People will exclude you when you crave acceptance.

You cannot spend the rest of your life being crippled by feelings of inadequacy; therefore, you will have to accept, hard as it is, that your position in society has changed. You cannot change the way people think about you, and so you will have to change the way you think about them. You will have to accept that some of the people you always thought you could rely upon for support and love are going to distance themselves from you. It is a kind of natural selection; the people with the strongest moral fibre, the people with true regard for you and your welfare, will stay with you. You may be surprised by exactly who those people turn out to be, but know that they will be your salvation when things get rough. You shouldn't concern yourself too much with those who fall by the wayside – concentrate your love and your time on those who deserve it, and forget about the rest. It is their loss, not yours.

But, having said all that, there are some people you can't just forget about. Close friends are especially important to you once your partner has died. If you have children, then you will instantly recognise the need for their godparents to step into the breech and take on the role of providing moral guidance. As a widow you will also be desperate for your children to retain some kind of male influence in their lives, and will therefore expect the people who were close to you and your late husband to provide help and support. But what if this doesn't happen?

Many of the letters I have received concern the subject of desertion and withdrawal. People write to me in disbelief and confusion because certain individuals they had assumed were close friends have failed them in some way. This desertion is very hard to take when you are at your lowest ebb, and will only add to your feelings of worthlessness and isolation. But the actions of others should not be seen as a failing on your part. To understand why some people choose to withdraw from us, we must first look at what drew them to us in the first place. If the people concerned were friends of your late partner before you met, or had a particularly strong relationship with him or her, then they will be going through a grieving process of their own. Seeing you may very well exacerbate their feelings of grief and loss, and therefore they may choose not to see you. I'm not saying this is right, but you have to understand that people do act in very strange ways when first faced with death.

There is also the problem of jealousy and, as I have already mentioned, you may well be seen as a sexual threat. Women are very wily when it comes to manipulating their partners, and even though you may pose absolutely no threat, you may well find that you start to see less and less of some of the people who mattered to you most. Some people will fall away from you and others will remain true – such is life; but as long as you remain true to those who have stayed with you through the worst of times, you can do no more.

party time

I have advised you to avoid formal dinner parties in the early weeks, but you may now feel ready for the odd party. Parties are easy – lots of people, dancing, food. Right?

Wrong.

I would not wish to put you off attending social functions, because you need to get out and have a relaxing, enjoyable time every once in a while. But I must caution you that what you hope a party might be – and what it actually is – can be two completely different things.

Josie Arkle had a most enlightening introduction to the joys of socialising as a widow . . .

I was invited to a friend's 50th birthday party, complete with Elvis impersonator, who I must say was very good. In fact, he was so good I was quite happy to sit and watch him. However, a lady I vaguely knew decided to take pity on me when it came to the slow dances (although I was quite happy sitting there, watching Elvis). She decided to ask me for a slow dance!

I insisted I was fine, didn't like the song, and would actually like to watch Elvis, but she wasn't taking no for an answer!

God it is so awful slow-dancing with another female. Maybe if I had a purple rinse and it was a tea dance but please, not this.

Eventually my neighbour came along and said he felt he had to join us as it just didn't look right! I assured him it didn't feel right as I didn't know where to put my hands, and I'd be more than happy for him to carry on the dance with my partner!

If you go to a party on your own, you will either have to use public transport or drive yourself, and driving yourself means that you cannot drink more than a glass of wine all evening. You will get used to this over time, but being sober as opposed to happily drunk does mean that you will remember any regrettable incidents with painful clarity the next morning.

Arriving at a party as a lone woman has to be experienced to be believed. If your hostess is a good friend then she might well meet you at the door and take you over to some nice people who will talk to you, but if it is a big party then the chances are that you will have to brazen it out alone. If the other guests are all good friends then it will be a fairly easy job to join a group and get chatting. Hopefully, this will make the start of the evening a painless affair, but even if you do know people at the party, there might still be a chance that someone has not heard your news, and so will ensue the inevitable explanation, followed by condolences and then a long, long silence as people struggle to think of something to say. At best you will change the subject with a witty aside and all will be well; at worst they will find an excuse to walk away, leaving you stranded in the middle of the room – and I'm not making this up, it has happened to me.

If you are among strangers, then somebody is bound to ask where your partner is. I can almost guarantee that it will happen at some stage during the evening, so you should be prepared with a stock answer to ease their embarrassment. I sometimes get bored with beating about the bush and come straight out with it – it is sometimes less painful for both parties that way. But as a rule of thumb, if you answer all questions relating to your partner with 'Actually, I'm a widow/widower' then you should be able to cope with most eventualities.

If this is your first party as a widow, you might well be struck with an overwhelming feeling of isolation. Even if people have been keeping you company for a while, it is likely that they will drift away from you at some stage during the evening, leaving you on your own. Looking around a room full of unfamiliar faces and wondering what to do next will induce a combination of nausea and mild panic, because there is nothing like a crowded room for making you feel totally alone. You have been cast adrift without the familiar life raft that was your partner; you may not have talked to him much during parties, but you always knew he was there. He was there to rescue you from boring conversations, he was there to listen when you wanted to whisper some salacious gossip, and he was there to take you home when you had had enough. Having him there gave you confidence, a reference point – an anchor. Not having him there will make you feel like drowning yourself in the punch bowl.

Arriving as a lone male might be considered a little easier, but it isn't. Your wife will have remembered everybody's name and will have steered you around the room, navigating you past all those people you really disliked and found interesting and engaging people for you to chat to. She would give you a look when she thought you'd had enough to drink and then she'd drive you safely home. Now you smile and joke and say you're doing fine; you eat canapés and sip champagne and then you come home to an empty bed and realise that you're not fine at all. All that bravura ends when you close the bedroom door, but nobody will ever know that except you.

Parties are not just difficult – they are fraught with danger. Consider a Christmas party I was invited to a few years ago . . .

The evening started pleasantly enough. I was given a lift by a friend, which meant that I could drink. There were lots of people I knew in attendance; I could socialise, eat nice food and dance the night away. It had all the makings of a great evening. And indeed it was a great evening until the disco started and I was asked to dance by an old friend. I had spent a while chatting to him beforehand; he had asked me how I was doing and I asked about his new baby, so it seemed entirely natural that we should dance together.

After the first record finished I turned to leave, but he asked if I wanted another dance. It seemed churlish to refuse and so we continued dancing, two feet apart and smiling at each other occasionally. And then all of a sudden I was being shoved sideways off the dance floor by his wife, who made sure that I was well clear before flinging her arms around his neck and rubbing herself up against him like some bonobo chimpanzee.

I wasn't sure whether to cry or throw myself into the speaker stack. I felt completely crushed and I wanted to leave – but I couldn't because I didn't have a lift home. And then I found that I couldn't get a taxi either, so I had to stay at the party and act like nothing had happened.

I had to try to hold my head up and act like I didn't care that I had been utterly humiliated. I had to share the same room with a woman who was looking at me like she'd triumphed over me in some way, like she'd won back the man I'd been trying to steal away.

I don't go after married men – she knew that.

Eventually I was offered a lift home by someone who turned out to be less than sober, and all I could think on the way home was, 'This is it, I've just been humiliated by an inebriated trollop and now all my friends think I'm after her husband. And why would I want to go after a man who considers the height of sartorial elegance to be a purple crushed velvet suit? Why would

I? And now I'm going to die in a Nissan Micra and it's Christmas and my children will be orphans.'

But I did get home eventually and my children did enjoy Christmas.

But I didn't forgive that woman.

And the moral of this story is – expect the unexpected. Don't rely on lifts – always try to drive yourself, just in case something does go wrong and you need to get home in a hurry. Do watch out for jealous wives, especially if they have been drinking. And if somebody hurts you, don't let them see they've hurt you.

Revenge is a dish best eaten cold. It took me two years of waiting, but I got mine eventually.

~

In summary

- You are a social leper.
- You will be viewed as a potential sexual threat – and even if you look and dress like Mother Teresa you'll still be seen as a marriage-wrecker in a wimple.
- Don't expect to be invited to dinner parties. The social invitations will dry up and you'll begin to feel about as popular as a foreskin at a Bar Mitzvah.
- At parties, somebody is bound to ask where your partner is. Honesty is the best policy, but don't expect the person to stick around for long once you've told the truth. You'll be left standing in the middle of the room, with only cheese and pineapple on a stick for company.
- Consider taking pocket solitaire or a Rubik's cube along to ease the boredom. You may look like a geek, but at least you'll have something to do, other than looking at your feet or admiring the wallpaper.

■ Going out alone is a lonely and depressing business, so make sure you have a car or taxi nearby so you can make an early exit if necessary.

■ It takes a huge amount of courage to go out alone, but drinking too much will not help you overcome your fear; it will only make you loud, embarrassing and then desperately tearful.

■ When you get home, your bed will offer no comfort to you. It'll feel big and empty and you'll feel upset and alone. But going out socially is part of the recovery process, and one day you will find that you don't really mind it at all.

Spine

The weather this week has been rather curious – cold and blustery one day, hot and humid the next. On Monday, when the sun bathed my garden in unseasonably oppressive heat, I began to long for a shady place to sit and swing. There's nothing I love more than to doze and dream away the afternoon – there are a million things to do inside, but when there's the promise of a crafty snoozle, the ironing pile can wait.

Putting up the garden swing seat is a job for two people; there are heavy wooden struts to manoeuvre and a bench seat to be brought down from a high shelf in the barn, but I couldn't be bothered to wait for assistance and so I man-handled all the pieces out into the garden and put it together myself. Getting out the garden swing heralds the beginning of summer, and each time I do it I think to myself, 'This is the last time I'll have to do this alone.' I have the same thought when I light up the woodburner to keep away the first misty breaths of autumn, and when I take down the Christmas tree

---

and fill the sitting room with pine-scented Hoover food. But so far I've just had to manage on my own, and for the most part it's really not so bad.

When people come to my house and see what I've managed to achieve single-handedly, they invariably make the same comment, which goes something like this: 'You're so competent and practical – I don't know how you're ever going to find a man strong enough to take you on.' And I smile and shrug, and mutter, 'Oh, I know there's somebody out there for me.' But all the while I want to take the well-meaning person firmly by the shoulders and shake them, while yelling in their ear, 'Don't tell me that! Don't you know you're mentally condemning me to a life alone? Don't you realise that I don't want to be this competent, practical person; that I want to be cared-for and cosseted. Don't you know I have 100 recipes I would love to cook, a dozen dresses I'd love to wear, perfume and jewellery on my dressing table that I've had to buy for myself? And I don't want to buy it for myself, just as I don't want to chop logs or put up the cockadoodie swing seat, but that's my life, and until a man comes along to help me I'm just going to have to make the best of it.' (You can see now why I don't get too many visitors . . .)

But my point is this: when people tell me I'll never find a man strong enough to take me on, what they are saying is that all English men are saps and wimps and sarong-wearing nancy boys, and I don't believe that. I don't believe that this country is peopled by emasculated men who are too brow-beaten and confused to be true to their sex. I have to believe that there are still a few men out there who are not frightened by a competent woman who knows her own mind. Where are the balls? Where is the grit? I know men are unsure of their role in society – they don't know whether to be hard or soft. Well, I know which I prefer, and I will not write off the entire male population of this country until I've been out with each and every one of them. Which leaves me with a slight problem – finding a man to take me out . . .

It seems there may be a solution to my predicament. I'm considered to be a forthright woman, so maybe I ought to re-examine my approach to dating, and also address my wardrobe. Maybe I would be a little more successful if I employed a couple of old-fashioned principles, namely wearing a skirt and not speaking. If I wear a skirt then hopefully the man I'm with will be rendered helpless with desire, and, if I refrain from speaking and let the man do all the talking then he'll feel really good about himself, and think that my enthusiastic nods and nervous giggles are due entirely to his charm and wit, rather than the fact that I've just had my jaw wired together.

But what if the date were a roaring success? Would I have to live a lie and pretend to be a meek, monosyllabic little mouse? Or could I use the second date to introduce some ribald humour and perhaps some light political discussion? Personally speaking, I think if you start out trying to hide who you really are, you are basing your future relationship on a lie, and as honesty and integrity are fundamental to me, I think I'll have to reject the skirt/mute idea in favour of being myself.

Being myself can be problematic at times, and one horribly memorable dinner party actually ended up like a scene from a Bateman cartoon. It was a formal dinner, given by a Rear Admiral – the details are unimportant, but suffice to say that Charlie was a long way down the table and therefore unable to keep me in check. I was seated next to a Major General, and we had begun an enthusiastic discussion about Sir Winston Churchill. I was keen to show that I knew my history, and gave my opinion of Churchill, which ended with the line, 'He was a pretty amazing man, but he seriously cocked up at Gallipoli.' I was referring to the First World War battle at which the Turkish army inflicted horrendous casualties on British and Anzac troops; I thought I had made a simple, yet pertinent point, and I couldn't understand why the Major General was choking on his beef and the Naval Captain to his right was trying to hide under the table. And then I looked to the end of the table and remembered that the guest of honour was none other than the Turkish Naval Attaché. Luckily for me he was seated out of earshot – his wife heard what I'd said, but she seemed to be following advice by wearing a skirt and saying nothing.

I don't think I delighted the Turks that evening with my horrendous faux pas, but the Major General soon forgave me, and I ended the evening sitting in the drawing room, drinking coffee, while the charming Naval Captain and the Rear Admiral sat at my feet. Not many chairs in the Royal Navy, but lots of lovely men.

So you can see why my score of dinner dates lies at zero, but at least I've been taken out to lunch recently. It wasn't a date, but a chance to catch up with my friend and wine merchant, Simon. I didn't have the heart to tell him that he was the first man in six years to have been brave enough to entertain me to lunch, but if I had done, I don't think he would have minded – after all, he's a real Englishman, and women like me don't scare him a bit.

19

portion control

widowers and sex

There is no getting away from it: at some stage you are going to have to start thinking about your sexual, as well as your emotional, well-being. For a man, sexual gratification is a fundamental part of life. Men are driven by their sexual desire; it is a primal urge and all women know that if you take a firm grip on the joystick of a vulnerable man, you can steer him just about anywhere you want to go. Therefore, there are two things that you, as a man, should try to consider before you start to look for female company.

First, you may well be seen as a soft target, a source of income for any calculating female who is callous enough to take advantage of your situation. If you are happy to get fleeced and fellated at the same time then go right ahead – it's your money – but try to consider your mental state and vulnerability. I know men do not like to think of themselves as vulnerable, but death can make the toughest man helpless. If you can try to hold on until a few months have passed, then you might avoid making a costly and permanent mistake.

It doesn't take a quantum physicist to work out that a newly widowed man is a prime target for marriage. You will be left craving female company, and this, coupled with your need for sex, may well cloud your judgement. The death of a partner can be devastating, but being stuck with a gorgon who sucks the money out of your wallet and leaves you with an IOU for pleasure is not going to help you when it comes to getting over your loss. I know of one man who was seduced on the day of his wife's funeral. This may seem unbelievable, but distraught widowers are an irresistible proposition to some less scrupulous women, and if a seemingly sympathetic friend suddenly throws herself at you, what are you going to do? What may only take five minutes has the potential to cause years of distress, so if you are tempted in a moment of weakness by the undulating bulges beneath your cleaning lady's housecoat, please try to look before you leap.

The other scenario we must consider is that you rush out and throw yourself at a woman who is as kind and loving as a girl can be, and then dump her because you're just not ready to commit. Yes, you deserve to be happy again, but if you have not yet come to terms with your loss, then you are going to make two people's lives miserable, instead of one. There are a lot of good women out there who long to have the attentions of a lonely widower, and much as you long for sexual gratification, you must try to consider the impact that your actions will have on the other person. You must also think about the impact your actions will have on the lives of any children you have. Your first duty is to them, and dragging them into a new and unfamiliar situation could be very harmful indeed.

I recently heard from a woman who had met a widower

through an Internet dating agency. It was only a couple of months since the man's wife had died and he had been left with two young boys to care for. The woman who wrote to me was worried about the children; although she loved her new boyfriend, she felt that his sons had not yet come to terms with the loss of their mother. Christmas was fast approaching and she wanted to know where I thought the best place for the boys would be at such a difficult time. I told her that I thought the best place for the boys would be at home, alone with their father. I personally felt that he had thrown himself into a new relationship before he had given himself and his children sufficient time to adjust to the loss of their mother. Christmas would undoubtedly be hard for all of them, but sometimes we all need an emotive occasion to prompt that which we have tried to bury and forget. I think that man was very lucky to have met a woman who showed such obvious concern for his well-being and that of his children. I'm sure that Christmas was difficult for them all, but if a woman can demonstrate that much thought for her boyfriend then I think that augurs well for their future together.

Robin Walker lost his wife to cancer at the age of 33. I asked him to write about his experiences following her death, and this is what he said:

A few months after Zoe's death I started a new relationship. This seemed shocking to many people at the time, including some of our close friends, who seemed genuinely upset. As a result we tended to keep the relationship separate from my previous life. In the first months the relationship was a great source of comfort and it helped enormously to have somebody to go out with, to talk to and to share things with again. I had heard of other men meeting somebody in the early stages of widowhood, and as it had worked for them I assumed this would work for me too.

What I have since learned is that you cannot easily replace what you have lost, that your situation places a large burden on your new partner, and that the chances of the relationship working out are not great.

The relationship worked well until around the first anniversary of my wife's death. My new partner thought I needed space and that we should have a 'time out' period. With hindsight this was exactly the opposite of what I needed, and at the time I also interpreted it as an attempt by my girlfriend to get out of the relationship without causing me further emotional trauma (it can't be easy to drop somebody who has just lost a partner). I responded badly and the end result was an acrimonious split, the repercussions of which dragged on for many months.

Tony, another widower, wrote this:

I realised very early on that I would be hopeless on my own. I have always enjoyed female company (although I was always faithful to Sally) and missed the companionship enormously. The prospect of having to 'get out there' horrified me – I never enjoyed it even when I was 18! While many of the problems this creates are, I'm sure, common to both widows and widowers, the one big difference is that it is the male who traditionally takes the initiative, thus adding further pressure.

Perhaps unusually, I met a single woman (by accident) only six months after Sally died and we have been seeing each other regularly ever since. This has presented a number of difficulties, some totally unexpected; some, no doubt, a result of the speed with which it happened.

Perhaps unsurprisingly, this has produced mixed reactions among my family and friends, some vocalised, some not (but nonetheless evident). Predicting the response has often proven hopelessly off-beam. Try as you might to take the attitude 'that's their problem', in the fragile emotional state one finds oneself in it can still hurt!

The reaction from my children has also been interesting. They have all (children and partners) given me massive support and, because of this, I was left wondering whether my actions are really causing them distress – even if they say otherwise. They obviously don't want to hurt me.

Judging how I really felt about my new partner has been difficult. However hard I tried not to, I inevitably drew comparisons with my wife. There was also a massive feeling of relief to discover that there was someone else out there I liked, who liked me in return. To further complicate things, when I am feeling 'down' at any particular moment, it is difficult to tell whether my sadness is linked with feelings for my new partner or simply a factor of grieving. On the other side of the coin, it takes a pretty strong woman to take on a widower and all that it entails. I talk to my partner very openly about my feelings, but it must still be very difficult for her at times.

Men tend to have a very pragmatic attitude to finding a new partner, and I believe that they look to female company as a way of helping them over their grief, often in the earliest stages of bereavement. A man will think, 'I need sex; I need someone to care for me; I need female company.' And he will go out and do something about it. Now, he may come to regret acting so hastily, but at least he will have done something positive. Men identify a need and they seek to fulfil that need. Job done.

DIY for widowers – the other sort

There's not much I can say on this subject, so I'll leave it to one of the widowers who has contributed to this book. I wrote to him, in all innocence, to ask about widowers' benefits and his reply was this:

'There's only one benefit as far as I can see – I can wank whenever I want.'

widows and sex

For women, the overriding need will be for protection and support – but that is not to say that a woman can do without sex. Sex and anger will go hand in hand, but on the whole, women seem to take much longer before they are able to contemplate being with another man again.

> The emotional make-up of a woman lends itself to long-term monogamy, and therefore the very idea of sex with another man may take some time to get used to. But eventually a woman's thoughts will turn to sexual fulfilment.

It took me quite a while before I could think about sex, but when I did, it was combined with a good deal of unresolved grief. I was full of anger and hurt and frustration. I had to get it out of me and I knew exactly how I would do it. I would have sex. Not in a romantic, Barbara Cartland way. No, I wanted it long, hard and rough – and I wanted it over and over again. And in my sad, deluded fantasy, when my staggeringly proficient lover would just be shutting his eyes for a well-earned rest after hours of sexual excess, I would prod him awake and tell him that I was ready to do it all over again. I saw sex as a release; as a bright, shrill whistle to let off the head of steam that was building up inside me. I was all ready to burst my rivets, and I thought if I could take a man and use him until I was completely exhausted, then that might help me get through my grief. But women are not traction engines; blowing off a bit of steam may have expended some of my excess sexual energy, but the complex emotional processes that go hand in hand with sexual gratification cannot be turned off at will. Once I'd let the driver pull on the whistle, I'd have wanted him to do it again and again. I would have expected him to call me, to text me, to think of me as more than just a mechanical object whose feelings could be steam-rollered in the rush for meaningless sex.

I have heard from several women who embarked on short-term relationships with totally unsuitable men in the early days of widowhood. There is nothing wrong with this, and I would not be sanctimonious enough to tell widows who feel the need for company that it is wrong to seek it so soon after the death of their partner. What a widow chooses to do is entirely up to her, and if the end result is a brief glimpse of sunshine in a dark, shuttered world, then I'm all for it. What I will say is that it may be a futile exercise, because the mind of a recently bereaved widow is not a model of rationality and restraint. You will do stupid things that you wouldn't have dreamt of doing in your right mind, and if those stupid things involve a man and his penis, then you could end up with a whole heap of trouble, and possibly a very nasty rash. The rash can be dealt with relatively easily, but the emotional scarring may take rather longer to heal.

I have to say that I'm not putting myself forward as the epitome of a successful man-trap. In fact, a widower of my acquaintance recently told me that I would be the last person he would come to for relationship advice – and he has a point. Six years have now passed since Charlie's death and I have yet to be taken out to dinner by an eligible man. I can't remember what it feels like to be kissed, and I have to spend a considerable amount of time in the men's underwear section of my local department store, just to remind myself what a man in his prime looks like without his trousers on. Sometimes the assistant in Debenhams lets me linger by the Calvin Klein underwear display. I stand in wonderment, gazing at all the fit male models, with the same look on my face that Homer Simpson gets when he sees a doughnut – although I try not to dribble quite as much. And then I trudge forlornly out of the shop while the assistant looks on with the kind of pitying expression that only a man whose merchandise has been handled a bit too often can truly muster.

But one day it will all be different; one day I will stride purposefully into the shop and demand a pair of Mr Klein's finest jersey boxers, soft and gently cupping, for the new man in my life. He will have the finest undergarments that money can buy and I will be able to walk right past the cardboard eye candy without so much as a backward glance.

I'm afraid my problem lies in the fact that I have the mind of a strumpet and the morals of Mother Teresa. I just can't do it. Try as I might, I can't just go to a bar and pick up a man and take him home for meaningless sex. It wouldn't be meaningless to me. Sex has to mean something. I have to feel something for a man in order to take him to bed. I would be letting myself down so badly if I were to succumb to my base urges and throw caution to the wind. And what about my children? What would they say if I were to bring a different 'uncle' home every week? It might keep me amused, but they would just end up getting hurt.

So I am left with a dilemma. How do I find a man? Well, I

think ultimately I'll find him by not looking for him. I'm going to keep on trusting my instincts and fate. I've stopped feeling lonely and desperate, and now I just feel like I'm maintaining a holding pattern until fate steps in and offers me up a prospective suitor – preferably one who wears tight, jersey boxer shorts . . .

DIY for widows – the other sort

What if you can't find a man? What then? It is impossible to talk about the trials and tribulations of being a young widow without touching upon the rather delicate matter of sexual release. The simple fact of it is that women reach their sexual peak in their mid-30s, which by some perverse twist of fate is exactly the time that many of us are widowed.

In an ideal world we would be able to go out and find a new partner, but being widowed in your 30s presents you with something of a problem. You are now too old to know many single men and too young to know many divorcés. That leaves married men, and I think they should be left well alone.

If you are lucky enough to meet a man when you have regained your sanity and your self-confidence, then that is fantastic. You will probably have the best sex you have ever had, buy a lovely house together and live happily ever after. If not, if you cannot find a suitable partner, then you will be presented with something of a dilemma. You will have thrown away all your old knickers and invested in lovely new underwear, with the expectation that you will find a man to appreciate it – and what? Nothing, that's what. All you have is a drawer full of pants and an empty diary, so what do you do now?

Well, let's approach this methodically. You are a normal, healthy woman, with a woman's needs. You have the following options:

a. Hire a male escort.
b. Join a dating agency and hope you meet a nice man before you become bankrupt.
c. Answer a lonely hearts advert in your local paper.
d. Pick somebody up in a bar.
e. Buy a device that will alleviate your sexual frustration.

I think a woman has to be pretty desperate to hire a male escort. First, they are extremely expensive. Second, have you seen the type of man who works as an escort? Third, if you did sleep with an escort, imagine how desperate, lonely and possibly very itchy you would feel when he left you the next morning.

Dating agencies have potential, but they can be really expensive.

Lonely hearts adverts in local papers are certainly an option; they are cheap, easy and undemanding, much like many of the men who place the ads. You might meet Prince Charming, but you might just as easily meet his ugly brother.

Picking somebody up in a bar has an element of danger that some may find exciting – so does wrestling a pitbull, but I wouldn't recommend either to a vulnerable widow.

And last but not least – that thing; that device; that unmentionable horror – the power tool.

Vibrator.

There, I've said it.

You know you shouldn't have to resort to such measures. After all you were attractive enough to find a perfectly nice partner. So what are you now? Desperate, that's what.

Other than sitting on your washing machine during a spin cycle or finding an enthusiastic and willing, licky Labrador, there are not many other ways of finding sexual release for a woman in your position.

Vibrator

There, I've said it again.

Purchasing such a device is never easy, and I can't think of anything worse for a widow than walking into a sex shop full of sad men and giggling girls shopping for their hen-night. You could try an Ann Summers party, but by far the easiest and most discreet way of finding what you are looking for is to buy over the Internet.

I'm not going to say any more on this subject because I feel that a woman's ladyparts are her own private kingdom, but I do hope you will find something to put a smile on your face – preferably something that doesn't have an economy wash or a waggy tail – but hey, if it makes you happy then who cares . . .

Seed

Today I went into town to get some bird food. Not very exciting, I know, but buying bird food passes for a big thrill round these parts. Anyhow, I went into the 'Everything Cheap Sold in Big Buckets' shop and said to the man, 'Have you got fat balls?' He looked confused and somewhat repulsed, and then I realised that he wasn't actually serving, but was helping himself to a bag of misshapen dog biscuits. Well, how was I to know? He looked just like the kind of man who sells fat balls in a bucket shop, and not the kind of man who owns a misshapen dog.

I have heard that shopping is a great way to meet a potential partner, but I don't think I want Mr fat balls in my life right now. I do like to engage people in conversation while I'm shopping, because I think most shop assistants need a bit of cheering up. I remember once strolling into an electronics hut at Calgary airport, and being approached by a most attractive young man. He said, 'Are there any questions that you'd like me to answer?' and I said, 'Yes, can you tell me the capital of Bulgaria?' He looked about as confused and repulsed as the fat balls man, and edged away from me as fast as his Crimplene slacks would allow. Well, I thought geography might make an interesting change from mega pixels and watts per channel, but he didn't seem to agree. I wanted him to see me as a witty, wry Englishwoman, but I'm afraid all he saw was an obtuse oddball.

I often look out for potential dinner dates when I'm shopping in Tesco's. I have to look in a man's trolley first, to gauge what kind of person he's likely to be. If I see cat food, tinned potatoes and athlete's foot powder then I tend to stay clear, but if there's fresh fruit, a decent claret and steak, then I know I might be on to a winner. Women can now view grocery baskets and use their contents to weigh up a potential mate – it's a bit like the cave girl instinct of looking at loin cloth length, but is much less likely to get you arrested for lewd behaviour. The most bizarre basket I ever saw being carried by a single man contained only two items: Head and Shoulders shampoo and K-Y Jelly. I don't know exactly which part of him was dry and itchy, but I didn't wait to find out.

It occurred to me today, as I was wiping the fatty residue of the birdseed balls from my hands, that perhaps the most dispiriting thing about being a widow is knowing that there isn't anybody who is thinking lovely thoughts about you. Friends give you an occasional call and relatives keep in touch, but the joyous thing about being a married woman is the knowledge that there is one man who has you on his mind all day long. You know that he's thinking about you while he's at work, and can't wait to get home to you each evening. That contact, both spoken and unspoken, is something to be cherished, and when you lose it, the silence becomes almost unbearable.

I used to get so overwhelmed by feelings of love for Charlie that I had to ring him up and sing to him down the phone. The choice of song was, perhaps, a little cheesy, but 'Andieeeeei Will Always Love Yoooooooouououou' was what I wanted to say more than anything. When the screeching became a little too hard to bear, he used to hand the receiver over to his PA, with the words, 'Whitney Houston – we have a problem . . .' But I think he was touched by the sentiment.

Charlie would call me several times each day for a chat, or just to see how I was, and I long for that kind of intimacy again. Nowadays, I'm pretty certain to spend my time at home in silence. I may get one or two phone calls, but more often than not I'll spend the whole day without speaking to a soul. This may account for my need to engage total strangers in conversation – admittedly I don't ask that many people if they have fat balls, but generally my opening line is something unusual. Perhaps I'm losing my mind. Perhaps all this enforced solitude has affected my precarious mental state and I'm turning into the strange eccentric that everyone expects me to be. But they just don't understand what it's like. They just don't have any idea how I long for a phone call that starts with the line, 'You've been on my mind all day.' Even a single, sexy text message would make me giddy with delight. I'm not expecting David Beckham's thumb to suddenly start throbbing with desire, but it would be nice to find myself standing in the queue at the post office some day, gazing adoringly at my mobile while absent-mindedly stroking a pair of rubber shoes, and then walking out, wondering why I've just purchased a box of Mr Kipling's exceedingly old cakes and a birthday card with a donkey on the front.

You can't buy that kind of attention. It doesn't come easily. It can't be found in a bargain bucket or a supermarket aisle. So where is it? Everyone's always telling me, 'It'll happen when you least expect it.' It is a phrase that's so easy to utter, and yet so terribly hard to hear. It's like being told that eternal happiness is just out of reach, but that if you screw up your eyes and pretend not to be waiting, it'll suddenly fall right into your lap. My lap is waiting; I'm relaxed and completely free of any expectation. So where's the fucking joy-bringer? Maybe I missed him. Maybe he was the guy at Calgary airport whom I frightened with my geographical brain-tease. Maybe he was the man with the itchy scalp and lubrication problem, or maybe he was the fat balls man. Maybe Mr Right is loitering just around the corner – but which cockadoodie corner?

I'm not expecting it. I'm really not expecting it. In fact, I've been not expecting it for the past four years. I've been not expecting a man to gently brush my hand as we both reach for the same mushroom bag in Tesco's; not expecting a lovelorn fan to write to me saying how much he admires my creative talents, and how he's spent the last year trying to decipher the secret messages hidden in the typos that litter my text. I'm not fucking expecting it, already. Are we clear? I'm ready now. My text thumb is poised; my husky phone voice is resonating deep within my chest.

Bring it on.

20

the perils of e-mail

I haven't always been so philosophical about my love life – there was a time a few years back when I was far more proactive and made a lot of mistakes. I grew tired of waiting to meet a man, so I decided to take matters into my own hands. This course of action led me to enter the wild and wacky world of Internet dating.

At this point I would sound a note of caution. If you believe as I did, that cyberspace is peopled not by social misfits, adolescent boys, married men and losers, but by normal, decent human beings, then you are wrong – because I have had e-mails from all of them to prove it. However, if you do wish to spend the rest of your life shackled to a bed in a trailer park on the New Mexican border, while Bubba (AKA Simon, the man who described himself to you in the chat room as an erudite businessman from Boston) lopes across the dusty ground, pulling behind him the small donkey that is to be your playmate for the entertainment of all his friends – carry on. Enjoy.

I had to find out for myself. I soon realised that chat rooms were not a place to meet a suitable man, but I did have high hopes for the Internet dating agency where I placed an ad. I had high hopes until I opened the first e-mail, and then I realised what I had let myself in for. I got messages from men all over the world, and I read them with the growing realisation that there are some really strange men out there whom I didn't want to meet – ever. If you need further proof, I will give you a small taster.

My first e-mail was from a man who finished his message of hope with the words 'I greatly enjoy giving women oral pleasure.' And my last was from a 52-year-old who told me that he stood 5'6" in his socks and weighed 64 kg 'without his clobber on' – his words, not mine. He went on to say, 'When I LOVE I LOVE DEEP!!' and finished, rather charmingly I thought, by offering a proposal of marriage and saying that before a firm commitment could exist, 'LOVE MUST cum into the equation.' I'm not sure if his spelling mistake was intentional or not, but I got the message loud and clear.

You, as a widowed person, should regard yourself as emotionally vulnerable, because that is what you are. And you should proceed with the utmost caution because you are not yet strong enough to suffer any further trauma, be it physical or mental. I am not saying that you shouldn't try to make yourself happy again, because that is the fervent wish of every person who has lost a partner in the prime of their life. You should be happy again – we all want to be happy again – but your happiness will be short-lived if you blunder into a relationship with the first person who lies their way into your e-mail affections.

E-mails are extremely dangerous because the written word is much more powerful than the spoken word. People say things in e-mails that they would never have the nerve to say to your face. People promise things on the page that they have no intention of honouring in real life.

You might find yourself pouring out all your troubles, all your hopes and desires to a man who, on paper, is more loving, caring, honest and sexy than you ever thought a man could be, but who is, in reality, a shallow, manipulative deviant who can't run off with you as he promised because he is married, has no intentions of leaving his wife and is only stringing you along for his own warped enjoyment. Or you could spend hours on-line, professing love to a stunning Kylie Minogue lookalike, only to find yourself sitting in an intimate wine bar face to face with Bernard Manning's less attractive twin sister. That, or you take months to find out that the long, delicate, perfume-scented fingers that type sweet nothings to you are in fact the pudgy, nicotine-stained digits of a desperate, lonely adolescent who has a good deal more facial hair than you do. You just don't know, so you have to be on your guard.

I am not being a prude, I am only trying to give you an example of what you might be letting yourself in for if you give away too much of yourself too soon. If you can bear to wait until you are strong enough to suffer a serious rejection, then you will at least have a chance of emerging from it unscathed. If you can find a date through conventional means, then at least you can see with your own eyes what you might be letting yourself in for. And if you can find some regard for your own abilities to make somebody fall in love with you again, after spending so long feeling totally worthless, then you deserve all the love that person can give you.

Although the Internet can be a dangerous place for both men and women, many people have found deep, lasting relationships through computer dating and chat rooms. Christine Myers wrote to me on the subject of cyber-dating . . .

Would you believe I met my husband via e-mail? The secret seems to be to avoid chat rooms/sites specifically aimed at 'dating'. I really wasn't looking for love – just new friends – and I got 'talking' to this man via a site on which it was made clear before you started whether people were looking for romance, sex with no strings or whatever. I signed up to the 'absolutely not interested in any of that stuff, just want someone to chat with' section, and within a few weeks was merrily 'e-chatting' with half a dozen people. One man in particular wrote great e-mails which made me laugh, held my interest and 'felt' honest. We e-chatted for a few months then he asked for my phone number which I nervously gave him. He told me some time later that he'd phoned me from a call box the first time in case I was a mad axe murderer who would trace him through his phone number! He spent the next hour coughing loudly every time he had to insert a coin – bless. After that we spent hours talking on the phone and decided there might be more to it. We met up and found we had 'chemistry', and here we are almost four years on and very happily married!

Spookily enough, my sister also met her fiancé via e-mail and is blissfully happy and getting married next year. I have to agree that there are an awful lot of losers, sex fiends, misfits and the like out there but there are some diamonds in among the rough.

But for every person who has found lasting happiness through computer dating, there is a multitude of vulnerable, lonely people whose lives have been ruined. What sets you apart from the other sad, lonely people who have set their hopes on finding love on the Internet is that you are a really attractive proposition. You have not been through a messy divorce that has left you all bitter and twisted. You are not a 40-something loner who's never had a serious relationship and who is now desperate to prove to his mother that the right girl really is a Vietnamese teenager who can cook and clean and dust the train set in the attic.

Widow or widower – you are a catch.

'Widow' says, 'I've got his life-insurance to tide me over, most of the mortgage has been paid off and I'm really lonely and longing for male company.'

'Widower' says, 'What's not to like? I'm attractive enough to have been married to a wonderful woman. I can provide for you. I need somebody to look after me. I need sex.'

> Don't put yourself at the mercy of people who are much more sad and needy than you are. Just think about it. Think about what an attractive proposition you are, and then start to value yourself a little more.

I'm not suggesting that you shouldn't indulge in a bit of harmless correspondence – after all, there is nothing more flattering than having a bulging 'In Box' – but just be cautious. It can become addictive, that feeling of excitement and anticipation. Coming home from work and knowing that someone's flattering words are waiting on your computer can become utterly compelling. I know. I know how much I needed to have a man to write the teasing, flattering words I craved, but my hunger for flattery was always tempered by my cautious nature; moreover, my close friends were always on hand to rein me back when they thought I might write something rash, or that I might be getting carried along by false hope. I am no expert on cyber-dating, but I always had a checklist, which helped me to avoid most of the weird, desperate men who were hawking their dubious wares in cyberspace. If you are a woman contemplating dallying with a cyber partner, then you might find it useful . . .

1. Avoid any man with 69 after his name if he isn't 36 years old – unless you are specifically looking for a sexually adventurous Lothario. I think, as a rule, men who advertise sexual positions are a little worrying; the same applies to men who have nicknames such as 'Iverbigun', 'GSpotTickler', 'Stalkerman' and 'Serialkiller'. One name I found particularly puzzling was 'Gonads'. How any man thinks he will attract a nice woman by using that particular pseudonym is beyond me. I can think of lots of male body parts that are worth drawing to the attention of lonely ladies, but those wrinkled, dangly portions should, I think, remain cloaked in mystery. He might as well have called himself 'Last turkey in the shop'.

2. Avoid any men who take photographs of their naked torso – and be especially worried if you can't see a face.

3. Avoid any men who include a photo of an erect penis – it probably belongs to somebody else, and it's way too much information for a first date.

4. I find pictures of men with waggy-tailed dogs on their laps distinctly worrying; and for me, any man who is pictured stroking a cat is right out of the question.

5. Avoid men who include a big, powerful motorbike in their photo. I love motorbikes, but it smacks of trying too hard. The

same goes for a man who is pictured standing beside a Porsche – any man desperate enough to wantonly flaunt his horsepower is bound to be lacking in other departments.

6. Avoid any men whose photos are in sepia, or include a Raleigh Chopper bike or a Stretch Armstrong action figure. Men often send in old photos, and you may get a nasty shock on your first date when the handsome man in the trendy flares and tank top turns up dressed from head to toe in M&S beige with mushroom accents, and spends the whole evening talking about the joys of a Baltic cruise and how the Adjustamatic bed has completely changed his life.

7. If you don't trust the photo, then you can sometimes tell the age of a man by his name. Derek, Dudley, Donald, Cedric, Arthur and Albert are all names of a certain era, but if you like tea dances and antimacassars then a Cedric might be just the man for you.

8. If the man in the photo is wearing a shell suit or a football shirt, and you wear a headscarf and green puffa jacket, then you can be pretty sure he's not going to be your ideal match.

9. Avoid any man who includes a picture of him holding a Thermos flask.

10. Avoid any man who posts a picture of just the Thermos flask.

11. And lastly, try to see through the pictures and the flattering descriptions; always remember what motivates many people to use the Internet for dating purposes – anonymity and escapism.

Having recently researched some Internet dating sites, I can honestly say I am amazed by the photographs some people use to advertise themselves. Amid the myriad photo booth shots there is always an occasional gem. Images that stand out from all the others – the man kneeling down behind a garden table laden with small, dead course fish immediately springs to mind, as does rusty pipe man . . .

I cannot reproduce the winning picture for fear of offending the man in question, but I'm going to describe it so you can get an idea of just how special this particular man was. He was pictured standing in the drive of a bungalow with one hand proudly resting on the petrol tank of a large, powerful motorcycle. 'What's wrong with that?' I hear you ask. Well, firstly, the motorcycle was old and exceedingly scruffy, with four rusty exhaust pipes thrust to the fore. When I saw the exhaust pipes, all I could think was 'personal hygiene problem'. If he hasn't bothered to clean his pipes, what else has he neglected? 'But you're just being picky,' I hear you say. Well, maybe, but let me continue before you make up your mind. The man standing by the motorcycle was sporting a pair of huge aviator sunglasses, circa 1977, and had teamed his retro look with a stained, navy blue sweatshirt, accented by black socks and dirty white trainers.

He was standing in a slightly unusual way (ballet third position), but there was nothing too disturbing about his appearance until you let your eyes rest upon what lay between the socks and the sweatshirt. Mr rusty pipes was obviously intent on displaying what he saw as his greatest asset, and to that end had hitched up his sweatshirt on one side to reveal a pair of black lycra shorts. Now, it may well be that he was a keen cyclist or an amateur gymnast, but his bulging waistband seemed to suggest otherwise. Frankly, I was worried by the contents of those shorts. I don't know what he had in there, but whatever it was, it clearly hadn't been let out for some considerable time. The picture should have been titled, 'Look at my tackle, and be afraid, be very afraid . . .' I was afraid – afraid for the safety of any woman willing to take on a lonely *Star Trek* fan with rusty pipes and a whole new way of storing spare socks. But one woman's nightmare is another's dream date, so what do I know?

The Internet. It's a dangerous place, full of sharks, so swim with caution . . .

21

diy

diy for widows

So what do you do with all those long winter nights? How do you occupy the hours that you used to spend in conversation with your husband? All those hours you spent cooking for him, mending the holes in his jumpers and ironing his clothes? Well, if I were to give you one piece of practical advice to help you cope with the everyday realities of being widowed, it would be this: get yourself a tool kit.

If your husband had a tool kit then dig it out and familiarise yourself with its contents; if he was totally impractical then you will have to get yourself some tools of your own. Television is saturated with DIY programmes that make it all look so easy, but the fact is that hanging a door or tiling a floor are jobs that take quite a lot of skill. I am not suggesting that you attempt anything complicated yourself, but there are some basic tasks like wiring a plug or hanging shelves that you can do yourself, thus saving the expense of calling in a carpenter or an electrician.

There is no need to go mad; you don't need anything fancy like a router or a circular saw, just a few basic essentials. The best thing to do first of all is to visit your local DIY superstore and have a walk around. You can ask for advice, and if you explain your situation then I'm sure the staff will fall over themselves to help you. You don't have to spend a fortune – most of the tools can be bought second-hand if need be – but the basic tool kit I would recommend is as follows:

- A claw hammer
- A pair of pliers (pointy)
- A pair of pliers (blunt)
- A Stanley knife
- A set of screwdrivers
- An insulated electrical screwdriver
- A saw
- A pair of wire cutters
- A set of spanners
- An electric drill – preferably a hammer drill
- A spirit level

I would suggest that along with your tool kit you also invest in a basic DIY manual. But if you only want to wire a plug, then most DIY stores have free leaflets, which explain how to do simple jobs around the house. Basic wiring is no more complicated than knitting, but people get scared when they think about electricity (I get scared when I think about knitting and I find wiring really easy, but then I never said I was normal). Anyway, if you are a complete novice, then start with a plug and see how you get on.

Before I get lots of letters from horrified safety officials, I must stress that I am not advocating that you gaily set about rewiring your house armed only with a screwdriver and a vague notion about the brown wire being live and the stripy one being earth. Electricity can kill, and so you must only attempt what you know you can do safely; but putting up a light fitting isn't rocket science – it just takes a bit of common sense – and with time, patience and application you will be amazed at what you can achieve.

> Knowledge is power. You can change a light fitting, you can mend a broken tap and you *can* assemble flat-pack furniture.

There are many unscrupulous tradesmen out there who will shake their heads and tut-tut when asked to do the simplest of jobs because they know you are ignorant and they can take advantage of you. If you can get a friend or neighbour who is competent at DIY to show you how to do some simple jobs around the house, then you will gain some level of independence. And even if you don't want to attempt any home maintenance, it is always useful to know how to find the trip switch, the fuse box and how to turn off the water stopcock in an emergency.

I have always been a very practical person, and after Charlie died I was driven to make substantial changes around the house. The first job I attempted was to redecorate the room in which he died, and since then I have gone on to do the following:

- Redecorate bathroom 1 and tile the floor
- Redecorate bathroom 2 and tile the floor
- Redecorate Rosie's room
- Redecorate Alice's room, rewire the lights, build bookshelves
- Redecorate spare room, block in a doorway, plaster, paper and paint the wall

- Redecorate my bedroom
- Remove carpet and fit a chipboard floor over the concrete floor in the study
- Wire lights in sitting room, fit oak window ledge, wax beams, paint walls and bookcase
- Fit stud wall in laundry room, build stand for Belfast sink, build cupboards under sink, box around lavatory, tile above the sink, fit tongue and groove panelling and redecorate

I completed all of the above jobs without assistance, save for my friend Beth ringing me up to tell me to stop at lunchtime and have a rest. I'm not saying that I'm some kind of superwoman; all I'm trying to say is that once you realise you have a talent for something, you don't necessarily need somebody to pat you on the back and tell you that you've done a good job. Doing a job and doing it well can be its own reward. You might think you have too much to do without having to worry about home maintenance, but there is a very good reason for getting acquainted with your tool kit. If you can master something you first thought was impossible then you will gain self-esteem, and self-esteem is something vital to your recovery.

N.B. As with anything regarding safety in the home, if you are at all unsure about what you are doing, then it is wise to call in an expert.

If you cannot be bothered with a whole box of tools, then you might like to consider investing in a 'Leatherman'. No, it's not a gay guy with buckskin shorts and a handlebar moustache – because frankly he wouldn't be any use to you, except perhaps for the purposes of running up curtains or teaching you the actions to YMCA. No, a Leatherman is a multipurpose tool, containing a saw, knife, pliers, wire cutters, scissors, screwdrivers and just about everything you might need in an emergency. There was a story recently about a man in America who was caught in a rockslide and became trapped by his arm under a boulder. He was miles from anywhere and unable to summon help, and rather than just give up and die, he took out his Leatherman and cut off his own arm. I cannot compete with that story, but I can testify to the sharpness of the penknife attachment, having recently lacerated several fingers in the course of using it to strip telephone wires. I think the 'Leatherman' is something that everyone who lives alone should consider buying. It's a damn sexy tool.

If you really cannot face picking up a Leatherman, then the other option is to pay for a home service agreement. Companies such as Direct Line Insurance now offer a complete home maintenance service, where, for a monthly fee, you can call out service engineers to fix just about anything in your home. It may be more costly then a tool box, but at least it will provide you with peace of mind in the event of an emergency.

Thumb

I thought I might start this entry by telling you about my injured thumb. I know you will be wondering what a digit has to do with your emotional well-being, but enlightenment will follow shortly – a bit like gangrene, or so the doctor said when he looked at what I'd done to my digit.

It is now six years since Charlie died, and apart from feeling a bit lonely on the anniversary of the day itself (strike that: terribly, terribly lonely and not a little desperate), I'm feeling pretty chipper. Spring is here, and at this time of year I always get a bit . . . well, a bit 'anxious'. The birds are singing, the sap is rising and I become filled with excess energy. My neglected libido could provide enough power to light a small conurbation. I am a walking Van de Graaff generator; sparks arc from my fingers, fluorescent tubes flicker into life when I pass.

I'm not abnormal; I'm anxious.

So, every year I am faced with the problem of how best to expend this excess energy. I did consider offering my services to Thora Hird as a human stair lift. I could be up those stairs carrying an old lady and a basket of cut flowers in a jiffy. And I would happily make the return journey, the flower basket now filled with dirty laundry, because this is real life and not a glossy advert (although I think the advertisers were sparing the viewing public by not showing an octogenarian coming down the stairs on an electrified throne, clutching a tangle of support stockings and crumpled pile of big pants).

Anyhow, back to my story. Over the past few years I have used my spring spurt to attack DIY jobs around the home, but now I find that I've done everything there is to do in my house; it all looks great, and so my attention has turned to the garden.

When the birds start to sing and the sun warms the primroses, I get an irresistible urge to be outside. My garden had lain neglected for months and was looking tired and sad, so I began to weed, pull, dig and edge like a woman possessed (imagine Charlie Dimmock on speed, but with appropriate undergarments – when she's working, why doesn't she get a bit of twine and a couple of plant pots and put those puppies away?).

Sorry, I'm going off the point a bit . . .

Once I had knocked the garden into shape, I planted out the vegetable patch with the help of my girls, and then we all stood back to admire our efforts. But it was no good. I still felt it – that itch, that gnawing, nagging feeling. So I cleared out my compost bin, rebuilt it from assorted bits of wood and then built a fence from scratch to hide my compost from the rest of the garden. Rosie helped me hammer in the nails and I began to feel sated. But still it wasn't enough. Once I had got going on the woodwork, my imagination took over and I resolved to construct a 'feature'. My garden needed a focal point and I would make it. Myself. With my tools. In my workshop. Did I wish Charlie was there to help me (not Charlie the bra-less bramble slasher, my late husband, Charles Boydell)?

No. I have long since stopped wishing Charlie was with me, for I know he is with me, and is watching over my every move.

I clearly remember the first DIY job I undertook without him. It was three months after his death and I decided to decorate the room in which he died so I could use it as my study. I sanded and waxed the beams, colour-washed the walls and made it look really lovely. And when I'd finished I stood back to admire my work and tried to feel happy. But I couldn't. I couldn't feel anything but loneliness and regret because I knew Charlie wasn't there to say, 'Well done, Katie.' I felt empty and alone.

Now I feel happy for myself; I feel happy that I've managed yet another difficult task unaided. My girls feel happy too, and proud of their mummy. They think I'm superwoman because they see me try. They see me struggle sometimes, but they never see me give up. To them I am mother and father; I am protector, cook, comforter, good cop/bad cop and television technician.

I am widow, hear me roar.

But back to the story: I decided to build a rose arch, so I got the instructions off the Internet, bought the timber and strapped on my work belt. It was all going so well; the first trellis was made, then the second, and then came the job of fixing the trellis to the posts. I had to keep the posts aligned while they were put into the ground and so had to nail on a big bit of timber to brace the two together. I got a big nail and began to hammer it home. It had to go though four inches of wood, so I was hitting it pretty hard. And then it happened; Charlie, my guardian angel, my watcher, my safety inspector, took his eye off the ball – or the hammer to be more precise. What he was doing God only knows. Maybe he'd wandered off to watch Elvis in concert; maybe he was taking tea with Princess Diana; or perhaps he was striding across the cloudy firmament with his puppy, Vicky, who knows? But whatever he was doing, he wasn't paying attention to me. The hammer came down, glanced off the nail and carried on to my waiting thumb.

I will spare you the details, but suffice to say it wasn't pretty.

After the pain had subsided I strapped up my thumb as best I could and carried on. Yes, I carried on. What would Charlie have said? Who the fuck cares? He wasn't paying attention in the first place and so I ignored the nagging voice in my head, turned up the volume on my iPod and let Kurt Cobain scrap it out with my reproachful husband. Luckily for me my friends Walker and Deb called round to see me shortly afterwards. They walked into the workshop and found me holding the hammer, and looking very sheepish. Deb was not impressed. She made me stop what I was doing and asked to inspect my thumb. Walker, big, butch man that he is, couldn't bear to watch, but Deb is made of stronger stuff. She winced slightly, but being an ex-nurse, she's used to seeing blood.

She did give me a very stern, disapproving stare and said she was exasperated with me, before applying herself to the task of re-dressing my thumb. Deb has now graduated from a nurse to being a very big noise in the health service, and having her put on a bandage is a bit like having your shoes polished by Jimmy Choo; but she hasn't lost it, although she nearly did when she saw that I'd been wielding a chainsaw earlier in the day . . .

So there it is. My Easter. The anniversary of Charlie's death passed without sadness, but with a good deal of pain. Life goes on and nails come off, but some things never change. Friends still stand by you, love you, and care for you in times of trouble. Despite carrying a grievous injury I still had to cook the children's supper. Jabbing my bad thumb on an upturned fork while loading the dishwasher really topped off my day, but my two little girls were there to hug me better. Spring is here; I have a thumb the size of a small watermelon and my life is full of hope.

diy for widowers

I don't think you need a woman to tell you how to put up shelves, and I'm certainly not going to tell you that you should be finishing all of those little jobs you never seem to get around to, because that would make me sound like a nagging wife, and I'm not. I'm sure you are perfectly able to cope with all the practicalities of maintaining your home, and I know that if there is something you can't deal with, then you'll get in somebody who can. All I would say is that you should be careful, because with no partner to tell you that you shouldn't climb a ladder without somebody at the bottom, or that you ought to turn off the power at the fuse box before you attempt to change a light fitting, you might well do yourself some harm. Just stop and think before you attempt anything too risky. Take a moment and listen to that voice in your head – you know, the one that reminds you of your partner. It will be her, telling you to be careful with the Stanley knife, or to unplug the drill – so be careful and cautious.

Muck

So the rose arch got made and my thumb began to heal, but still there was the tricky problem of having to erect the monstrous edifice I had constructed. It didn't look big and heavy in the plans, but it is. Big and heavy. I didn't relish the job of putting it in place, but I needed to get outside in the garden after spending the morning trying to find cheaper household insurance. The man on the phone asked for my marital status, and when I said 'widow' he said, 'Oh, I'm sorry.' And then proceeded to give me a much higher quote than the previous insurer, at which point I felt like saying, 'Well, you're not THAT sorry then are you?' After that I went to order some dollars from the bank, and as the helpful customer care lady began to fill in the form, Rosie turned to me and asked, 'How do you spell dollar?' I told her, and thought nothing more of it until I got home, looked at the form and realised that a bank employee had written the word dollor (sic), not once, but twice. Well, call me old-fashioned, but it's not the most taxing currency to spell correctly, is it? Had I been trying to order 50 quid's worth of Ngultrums for a mini-break to Bhutan then I might have forgiven such a slip, but really, she must have handled enough greenbacks in her time to know better.

Anyhow, back out in the garden I had enlisted the help of

my good friend Linda to get the rose arch into place. She did blanch slightly when she saw the size of it, but was eager to prevent me causing myself further injury by trying to lift it alone. Being an ex-nurse (yes, I know lots of them) she was also very cross with me for hurting myself yet again, and told me that she would take away all my power tools if I misbehaved in future. After considerable grunting and straining we eventually got the arch into place, and I have to say that it looked even bigger standing upright than it had done lying down (fill in your own gag here . . .). Linda looked at me, said, 'Better get some roses up it quick' and then made her excuses and left. This left me with the job of concreting the posts into place.

Mixing concrete isn't difficult; it's just tiring and messy. I'm now going to tell you how to do it, just in case you ever have to build a brick wall, or make some heavy footwear for a contract killing. And just so I don't put you off, I'm going to do it in the style of Nigella Lawson . . .

How to make muck
1 bag of cement
3 bags of chippings to dust (aggregate)
a quantity of water

First, get your bag of cement; take a really good quality shovel, grasp its thick shaft firmly and drive the head deep into the bag. The crispy brown wrapping should part with a satisfying rip, yielding forth the soft, pewtery Portland powder. Then do the same with the plastic bag that holds the aggregate, and place three heaped shovelfuls of the nutty, crunchy, gritty mixture onto a large board – hardboard is best, but if you can't find it at your local merchant's, then just use whatever comes to hand. Then take one shovelful of the thunder grey cement powder and add it to the aggregate. Mix the two together, and then make a well in the centre of the mixture. Take your trusty zinc watering can and let a quantity of water cascade from the proudly-jutting spout (rainwater is preferable, but if you can't get hold of it then you'll have to make do with Evian or Badoit). Gently introduce the mixture to the liquid by softly nudging the sides of the depression with the tip of your shovel, but be careful not to be too rough or you'll bruise the mixture. Once the liquid is amalgamated take your shovel and push vertically through the mixture using a backward chopping motion. Repeat with occasional lifting and dropping and turning of the muck until the concrete resembles a loose Dundee cake mix. The mix is now ready to use as a base for posts, but if you want to lay brick, then replace the aggregate with builder's sand.

N.B. Although the concrete mix does look just like cake mix, it is not advisable to lick the utensils clean after use.

~

I figure that if I can mix concrete then most people can. The arch is now held firm and I can begin the task of trying to hide it. Rosie made me a welcome cup of tea and saw fit not to pass comment, although I knew enough from her wry expression to recognise that she thought I'd constructed the folly to end all follies. She and Alice are back to school next week, and I will be able to resume a life of indolence.

Some hope.

I should rejoin the local gym – I did enrol a few years ago in the hope of meeting a sweaty, muscular quantum physicist, but gave up after I got fit and realised that the Bernard Manning lookalike in the headband and baggy sweatpants was the best that Devon had to offer in the way of a potential gym partner.

Such is life and, as I constantly tell myself, all good things come to those who wait.

22

holidays from hell

Question: What do people do to relax and unwind?
Answer: They go on holiday.

Question: What do widows and widowers do to get stressed out
and wound up?
Answer: They go on holiday.

I think it is safe to say that going on holiday alone, or alone with
children, in the early months of widowhood is the most desolate
and unpleasant experience imaginable. I can remember every
second of my first holiday alone with the girls with painful clarity
– and I wasn't even alone; I was with Charlie's family. But that
didn't matter to me; it was only three months after Charlie's death
and it was far too soon. Every single experience on that holiday,
which would once have been pleasurable and evocative, became
detestable. Only the happiness of my girls brought me any respite
from the black cloud that shadowed every balmy day.

When we first arrived at our French holiday home, I was overwhelmed by the beauty of the landscape, and then immediately by the knowledge that Charlie wasn't there to see it with me. I knew he would have loved it; I knew he would have taken over the kitchen and busied himself rustling up something delicious for supper, while we all sat on the shady terrace with a glass of wine and watched the sun setting over the distant hilltops. But none of that was going to happen. I was seeing it alone. I had nobody with whom to share the sights and the smells and the resonance of the place. By day, with Charlie's family and my children, I was alone. At night, while a thunderstorm lit up the shuttered darkness like a million flashbulbs, I was alone. I felt I should enjoy the holiday for the sake of my children, but all I wanted to do was get in the car and drive back to where I felt safe and protected.

When at last the holiday was over and I could return home, I vowed that it would be a long time before I ventured abroad again. And of course it was foolish to do that, because getting away from everything that helps you feel safe and secure is part of finding out about your strength and your ability to cope with the reality of being widowed.

My advice would be to wait a while before you go on holiday. If you can establish some sort of structure at home, then you will find it much easier to cope with the uncertainties of being a single traveller. When you feel ready to face it, getting away by yourself is great – but getting away when you are a lone parent is not always easy to do. Finding somebody to look after your children for a week is quite a tall order, but if you have friends or family who are willing to help you, then a week's respite from your responsibilities will do you a power of good.

holidays for single travellers

But where do you go and what do you do? Well, the Sunday papers are full of adverts for holidays for the single traveller. It is up to you which of these you investigate but, generally speaking, you can be as active or inactive as you like. Personally, I would rather cover myself in jam and sit on a termite mound than go on a trekking holiday, but many people enjoy that sort of thing. I love scuba diving because it doesn't involve stout boots or facial hair, but I know that many people find the thought of putting on a mask and going underwater to a depth of 30 metres totally abhorrent. What you choose to do is entirely up to you, as long as you feel safe and happy doing it, and there aren't too many weird people doing it with you.

I have enjoyed some really excellent holidays as a single traveller. My first holiday had to be a good one, and so I chose an activity I had always wanted to do but had never had the nerve or the money to contemplate before. The madness of widowhood had unlatched the door to my reckless nature, and so the first challenge I set myself was to leave my children for a fortnight (which would be an ordeal in itself) and travel to Canada, where I would be staying on a working ranch. Doesn't sound that adventurous, does it? But there was a catch – I had a fear of horses. This was triggered at the age of six by being dragged the length of a suburban cul-de-sac under the round, dappled tummy of a pony called Peppermint. My three sisters all managed to stay on Peppermint, and all went on to become excellent horsewomen, but I had to make do with a moped.

> Moose
> Throughout my life I have encountered a number of remark-
> able people, and the ranch owners, Lane and Margy Moore,

were no exception. We are often told that Canadians are a dull, humourless race, but Lane and Margy were anything but dull. Lane was a kind, gentle man, who had such an affinity with his horse that he could ride it without saddle or bridle. It followed him around like a faithful hound, and after two weeks on the ranch, most of the guests did exactly the same thing. Lane had married Margy shortly after the death of his young wife. Margy was a great cook and was always at pains to make me feel at home. She even made sure I had a good supply of reading matter in my room. There was a magazine called *Nuzzle* by my bedside, which I thought was some kind of weird Canadian horse-porn, but thankfully, it was just a publication for people who like riding – unlike *My Big Pony*, which can be found on the top shelf of our village post office, and brings a whole new meaning to the phrase 'struggling with your girth'. I must confess that I did have some rather disturbing dreams before I embarked on the riding holiday, but as Catherine the Great once said, shortly before being crushed by a two-tonne Percheron stallion, 'Don't knock it until you've tried it.'

Back at the ranch and I was having a simply splendid time. I can't ever remember laughing so much; Margy and Lane had the kind of sharp, dry wit that I love, and being in their company was like taking happy pills. There were times when I got tearful, but Lane knew exactly what I was feeling, and gave me space and time to be alone. Margy took me under her wing; she took me shopping to the local general store, which was a place of wonderment for a shy girl from Devon.

When I was young I used to love watching *Little House on the Prairie* – it wasn't the schmaltzy storylines or fine acting that held my attention, but the unspoken promise that one of the Ingalls girls might be asked to accompany her dimple-cheeked father on a trip to the general store. I watched in rapt attention, longing to be the pig-tailed girl with the overbite who got to ride on the bench seat next to the man with the badly-permed hair. One crack of the reins and a 'giddyup mule!' later and we'd be off, bouncing along the dusty track and over the hills into town.

The mercantile was a place of mystery and promise; it sold feed and grain, saddles and shovels, handguns and hard gums. That shop had everything, and I wanted it all. I wanted to walk through the door, passing as I did so a woman in a bonnet. It may have been my imagination, but she always seemed to be in the shop, holding a length of gingham cloth up to the light in order to check it for flaws and imperfections. So, after squeezing past her dusty bustle, I would stand and gaze around the sacks of maize, barrels of molasses and rows of picks and hoes, and then I would let my eyes settle on one of the large, glass jars on the high shelf above the counter. The sweetie shelf was always so enticing, but what I really wanted to buy with my shiny nickel was a cart full of implements, some seed corn, a big gun, a cowgirl outfit trimmed with suede, and a snorting black stallion. In fact, I wanted to be just like Laura Ingalls Wilder – only wilder.

We don't have a general store in our village, just a small post office, and much as I like to support local business, loading my wagon with a pair of rubber shoes, a dusty jigsaw puzzle and a packet of Happy Shopper digestive biscuits doesn't seem to fulfil my fantasy in quite the way it should. So, you can imagine my delight when I was let loose in a genuine Canadian mercantile.

My first impression wasn't so much Happy Shopper as bloodthirsty, sadistic and possibly quite deranged shopper.

The store's shelves were stacked high with everything you could possibly need to maim or kill a large mammal: guns, bows, knives – you name it, they had it.

Before you can kill a moose or an elk, you have to attract them, and you wouldn't believe the fiendish devices that Canadians employ to do this. I didn't know that elks had a musical ear, but they clearly do, because hunters use a thing called an 'elk trumpet' to get their attention. You could also buy a device called a 'lip bugle', an 'elk diaphragm', and if you got really desperate, a 'bull moose stimulator'. I was quite tempted to get one of those, but I chickened out because it was too expensive – and anyway, I'm not sure that even I could handle an overstimulated moose.

I wish now that I'd bought a gift to take back for my friend Beth; she works as a family planning nurse and I think it would have been an interesting little addition to her box of contraceptive devices . . . 'Didn't you get on with the Dutch cap? Well, how about trying an elk diaphragm?'

When we got back from the store, Margy and Lane decided to take me on a trip to the ranch's mountain camp, a small enclave on the banks of a winding river. The tents had wooden floors, wooden beds and a small woodburning stove to keep out the chill mountain air. There was a corral for the horses, a cook tent and wash tent, where you could put up a screen, stoke up a stove and get a piping hot shower when you needed one.

I spent four unforgettable days in the saddle, riding along steep mountain trails, spotting beavers, moose and grizzly bears, crossing icy rivers and galloping across vast tracts of open pasture. The days were long and the riding was hard; I was a novice among experienced riders and I had to keep up, but Lane was always nearby, keeping a watchful eye on me. We rode until lunchtime, ate our sandwiches in flower-strewn Alpine meadows with the horses tethered in the shade of nearby pine trees, and then mounted up and followed Lane as he guided us safely back along the trails to our tented mountain home. And as we dismounted at the end of the day, after six long hours in the saddle, I knew I felt truly happy for the first time in months. And sore. Oh, the soreness – I felt like one of the women out of *My Big Pony* magazine – and not in a nice way. But what a wonderful adventure; there is no sight quite like the Rocky Mountain sky at night. As I left the warm fug of my tent to take the night air, I looked up and gazed in awed disbelief at the limitless expanse of star-scattered firmament. Let me tell you, if you don't believe in God, just go to the Rockies at night and look up.

I believed in God that night; I believed that I could be happy again – and I also believed that if I didn't get back in my tent pretty sharpish, then a big bear might come along and gobble me up. But I wasn't really scared. I knew that somewhere up in the glittery blackness was at least one person keeping a watchful eye over me. He'd made sure I was safe in the saddle of my faithful steed Hazy; he'd placed me in the care of a kindly, horse-whispering widower, who'd found happiness and love among the pine trees of Alberta. He'd made sure I had good company, cold beer and a whole lot of understanding. I was in a good place. The Lazy M Ranch; first stop on the journey to my recovery.

I have been scuba diving in the Red Sea on a couple of occasions, which was excellent fun and good value for money. You will find lots of single travellers on a diving holiday – if you are lucky. If, like me, you expect to find a handsome instructor and lots of single men to buddy-up with, then you might be disappointed. I found myself a lone woman in a group of couples, being taught not by a tall, bronzed divemaster, but by a short, stout woman called Freddie Pickles. Now how lucky was that? To top it all off, when I got in the water I was greeted by a rather nasty and aggressive Titan trigger fish, which bit right through my fin and then chased me all the way back to the boat.

None of these experiences fitted with the cosy image I had of spending hot, lazy days on a dive boat, being chatted up by handsome strangers – but I did come away from the trip with my PADI Open Water qualification, and a love of diving. The next year I went back to get my advanced qualification; I got in with a group of divers who were mostly solo travellers, and we went out together every night and had a really wonderful time. I still had the inevitable awkward question to field, but when a diving chum asked if I had left my husband at home, instead of being tongue-tied, I just looked at him and said, 'Yes, I did leave him at home – because he died three years ago, and that makes it a bit difficult to bring him with me.'

It was also during that particular holiday that I learned of the five special places . . . I had wandered into a perfume shop in Sharm El Sheikh to buy some souvenirs to take back for my girls. I was hot and tired and it was nice to be out of the sun. I spent a while looking at the vast array of delicate, glass scent bottles that lined the walls of the shop, and became distracted enough for the young salesman to persuade me to stay for a cup of mint tea. Once he knew he had a captive audience, he proceeded to try out the classic Egyptian sales technique on me, which went something like this: 'My name is Ibrahim. Look into my eyes. You come for a drink with me tonight. I take good care of you. Look into my eyes.' I did look into his eyes, and it has to be said that they were dark and mysterious, but not nearly as dark and mysterious as his teeth. I had never seen so much dental detritus in all my life and it was all the incentive I needed to turn down his offer. After all, I didn't want to spend the evening chewing on a cheese and pickle sandwich I hadn't even eaten.

But though I wasn't falling for his patter, I was rather interested when he told me about the special powers of one of his fragrances. He brought over a large, glass bottle, pulled out the gilded stopper and then rubbed a small amount of the scent into the cleft of my elbow. I have to admit that it smelled divine. It was heady and intoxicating, without being sweet and cloying, as so many perfumes tend to be. I asked what it was called. 'Secret of the Desert' contained marihuana, among other things, and was undiluted by alcohol, so it was a pure essence, and not simply a perfume.

Ibrahim could see I was interested, so he hit me with the killer line, 'This fragrance is special. It make a man like a horse, and he go for seven hour.' SEVEN HOURS! I had visions of men snorting and pawing the ground; of creaking leather and the smell of saddle soap. I had visions of peppermints and slices of apple on the bedside table; and of long, long winter nights lost in the heady, dopey thrall of that exotic, golden essence. But there was a catch – the fragrance would only give a man certain equine qualities if first applied to the five secret places on a woman's body – places that all Bedouin women are apparently familiar with, but which, Ibrahim told me, none of his European customers had so far guessed correctly. What was wrong with European women? Didn't they know what they were missing? Well, Devon maids know a thing or two, and after giving it a bit of thought, I managed to guess all five correctly. I said goodbye to Ibrahim, and left the shop with a large bottle of the mystical potion.

I had it. I had the 'Secret of the Desert'. Now all I needed was a man to try it out on . . .

When I got home I told a couple of my female friends about this wondrous fragrance. They were equally enamoured, and begged me to purchase some for them on my next trip to Egypt. I did as I was asked, and although I have yet, personally, to find a man to attest to the efficacy of 'Secret of the Desert', I can report that one of my friends has achieved quite spectacular results with her husband, and is now considering changing his name to Mr Ed.

(Oh, just in case you're wondering about the five 'special' places – here they are: the pulse points on either side of your neck, the cleft between your breasts, in the crooks of your elbows, the backs of your knees, and lastly, if you think of the other places as signposts to the final destination, number five *is* the final destination . . .)

~

I have learned a lot from going on holiday on my own. It takes a lot of courage, but then if you don't try, you never get to test just how far you have come. I'm not going to try to tell you any of this is easy – it isn't. There have been many times when I wanted to feel happy about where I was, and whom I was with, but all I could feel was, 'Why isn't he here to share it with me?'

It makes you cry with frustration and loneliness, but it does get better in time. I have travelled a long way, and not just on aeroplanes. I have set myself difficult tasks and watched myself grow with the completion of each one. You might not feel confident enough to contemplate travelling alone, and I would certainly not recommend even thinking about doing so for at least a year after being widowed, but just thinking about going away alone is half the battle.

Whether you choose to travel alone or in a group of solo travellers, you will be taking the first steps on the road to independence. Nobody wants to be alone; it is depressing and soul-destroying to look at a calendar and see nothingness stretching ahead of you, but if you have something positive to look forward to, and something to work towards, you are less likely to dwell on the negative aspects of your life.

holidays with children

Going away with children is a different thing entirely. Basically, as a rule of thumb, expect all mainstream travel companies to penalise you for being widowed – as if you didn't have enough to deal with. Even the ones that say they have special offers for single parents make up the extra money on the discount they have been so very generous in giving you by charging you a single supplement on your room for each day of your stay. They are quite blatant about it, in a sneaky and underhand way (it's all hidden in the small print, if you know where to look). I found out about the dubious practices of holiday companies when I took Rosie and Alice abroad a couple of years ago. When I got to the hotel I discovered I was paying £300 more than a couple with one child, who were staying in exactly the same type of accommodation for the same amount of time. How does that work?

My advice is to be very careful when choosing who you book

with, and don't expect them to feel sorry for you and offer you a discount just because of your circumstances.

Booking the holiday is only the first problem you will encounter. The journey – be it by ferry, car, rail or plane – will be stressful and tiring. When you have nobody to share the driving or help you with all the mundane essentials, life becomes extremely difficult. Even a simple task like taking one of your children to the bathroom will become almost impossible. Where do you leave the luggage trolley? What do you do with your other children? How do three smalls and an adult all fit into one cubicle? Well, the answer is you learn only through trial and error. I can guarantee that you will find the whole thing a complete nightmare from start to finish, and you will definitely need a holiday at the end of it.

Holidays with your children are like weekends – magnified tenfold. As a widow on holiday you have to be around men; men who are making a special effort to be perfect fathers, and that will make you feel very jealous, and will make your children feel the loss of their own father even more acutely. By the same token, if you are a lone father, then people will assume that you are a divorcé. They will make no allowance for the fact that your children will be distressed when they see other children being hugged and cosseted and carried by their mothers. But you have to bite the bullet eventually. You know your children deserve a break, and it's only for a week or two, and how hard can it be?

Very hard . . .

If you have booked into a hotel on your own, the days will be spent by the pool or on the beach, which isn't really too difficult to cope with. But there will be one nagging fear, which will pervade your happy holiday state of mind, and that is: what do I do once the children are in bed? The answer is that you have to walk into a packed dining room alone, sit down alone, eat alone and leave alone. I have done it, and in terms of memorable dining experiences, it's way up there with eating a bad oyster and being stuck next to a man who told me he was 'in lubricants' and spent his spare time as a small-gauge railway enthusiast.

Two years ago, for instance, I sat in a dining room at a table for two and ate my supper alone. I felt fine until I noticed the unwelcome attentions of a German woman who was seated at the next table. She stared at me for the entire duration of the meal, and for the whole of that meal I was looking out at the sunset, trying my best to ignore her, but willing her to choke on a big, fat olive stone.

It wasn't so hard, but I couldn't have done it in the early years of widowhood. Everything takes time, and some things take an awful lot of courage; so don't do anything you don't feel brave enough to take on. Don't go abroad if you can't face it, or you can't afford it. Do something simple like taking the children camping. Even if it's just in the back garden, I can assure you that they will see it as a big adventure; they won't care where they are, as long as they have you to share the experience with them.

Urn

Today, in light of the appalling weather, I have decided to continue my holiday horror stories. I will start with a trip to the Greek island of Lemnos, which was the first holiday the girls and I took alone. I thought it would give me a break and I hoped my daughters would get to experience the beauty of the Greek islands. But the island wasn't remotely beautiful; it was barren and bleak, with a large military base and lots of dry, brown scrubland – oh, and some goats.

It was a fairly uneventful holiday; I sailed a bit, swam a bit, and got a salt water enema courtesy of the waterskiing instructor. The girls had a whale of a time, and made full use of the excellent activities provided by the kindly blue-shirted staff. I tried my hardest not to look too out of place among the plethora of upwardly mobile families, but in the end I had to admit defeat and brazen it out as the only single woman there. One couple were kind enough to befriend me; they ran a well-known accident claim company. The wife appeared on their television commercials, although I failed to recognise her on the occasion of our first meeting because I was concentrating on trying not to trip over with a bucket of hot tar . . .

I can't say any more about the holiday than that. The beds were hard, the sea was wet and the sun shone. End of story.

The next year my in-laws agreed to accompany me to Crete. It was an experience that made me determined never to travel with this particular holiday company ever again. The hotel was expensive, but made even more so for the single parent. (Here's a tip if you are travelling with children: book one of your children as an adult and you will save a fortune in single supplements.) The sea looked so inviting when we arrived, but we soon discovered that the reason there were five pools in the hotel grounds was because the beach was too dangerous for swimming. There was a very strong swell most days and a nasty undercurrent. Coupled with that, the shore-line appeared to be constructed from uneven concrete, which made the prospect of falling over less than desirable. I felt terribly guilty as I had been the one who had chosen the hotel, but I do think that the holiday company should have mentioned the dangerous beach in their glossy brochure – in fact, I'd like to write the entry now: 'Lovely pools, occasional aggressive English lounger-grabbing yob, good food, nice rooms overlooking the dustbins, lethal beach with dangerous swell and deadly undercurrent that will pull the feet from under your children. And lastly, helpful reps who insist on using the term "miself" in every sentence; for example: "If you have a problem, come and see miself, and either miself or Darren will try to help yiselves to sort it out. And to finish our welcome meeting Darren and miself would just like to add that you can get maps, guidebooks, postcards and a bad case of chlamydia from miself or Darren, which will be a lovely reminder of your holiday."'

After a week at the Dangerous Beach Hotel, the rest of my party returned to England and my girls and I were left alone. We did manage to strike up an acquaintance with a lovely couple from Devon, and that at least made the second week more bearable. I think the highlight of our stay had to be the night I awoke with a two-inch cockroach crawling across my naked stomach. I managed not to scream, captured the creature and put it under a glass in the bathroom. The next morning I put it in an envelope and took it to reception. When I showed it to the receptionist, he just shrugged and said, 'It's nature.' And that was it. No apology, no free meal, nothing. I didn't get cross, which I should have done, but neither did I tell the hotel staff that it was by far the most exciting thing that had happened to me in bed for many a long year.

I know I like to bang on about it, but holidays are hard when you're sad and single. I think we can all learn a lesson from my good friend Sarah. She's just about to go on holiday for the second year running with a couple of delightful gay men. Gay men are funny and kind and unthreatening; in fact they are the perfect holiday companions for any widow, and so my advice to anybody thinking of booking a late holiday is try to choose companions who like to go Greek . . .

Last year I decided to go for broke and take the girls on the trip of a lifetime. We all went to a ranch in Colorado, which was so eye-wateringly expensive that at one stage I did consider selling a kidney in order to pay for it. However, my extravagance proved to be worth every penny, because apart from having a wondrous time, during our second week we met a Californian family who managed to completely change my attitude to going on holiday alone. Not only did our children get along, but Gregg and Sharon Hartman proved to be just about the most entertaining couple I have ever met.

I have Rosie to thank for our introduction. She had fallen over during our first week at the ranch and had badly gashed her knee. As luck would have it, the ranch owner happened also to be an ER doctor, and he stitched Rosie's knee up on the porch of our cabin the very next day. The following week, the Hartmans arrived. Gregg noticed that Rosie was sporting eight stitches, and, being a kindly orthopaedic surgeon, offered to take them out. Once the ice was broken I discovered that I had been lucky enough to chance upon an American couple with a startlingly good grasp of irony, which is about as common as stumbling across a pair of welcoming Parisians or a really hilarious German.

We spent the whole week laughing; Gregg and Sharon asked me to accompany them on their rides across the prairie divide, and, for the first time since Charlie's death, I was made to feel like I really belonged. Before meeting the Hartman family, holidays with the children consisted of going into the unknown. I knew I would have to try to make friends with certain couples for the duration of the holiday, and it was always a lottery, because I never knew whether the parents of the children my daughters befriended would turn out to be entertaining or excruciatingly dull. It's different when you are part of a couple

– you can make an excuse to get away – but when you are alone you have nowhere to run. If you are asked to share a dinner table, what are you going to say? 'No, actually I'd rather sit alone and be stared at all evening by an annoying German housefrau.'

Sometimes it pays to put yourself out on a limb. I have made friends for life, friends who don't see me as a potential marriage wrecker or social liability; friends who are funny and smart and kind. God bless America.

In summary

- Holidays alone are hell.
- Mainstream tour operators penalise the single parent – don't expect a bargain when you see 'special offers for single parents' because they make up the money by charging a single supplement for every day of your stay.
- Many travel companies offer accompanied holidays for families and single travellers, which might be an attractive alternative to a beach holiday and will mean that you don't necessarily feel so isolated.
- People will view a single parent on holiday with a degree of suspicion.
- The mechanics of travelling alone with small children are a nightmare. Even the simplest task will seem impossible and you will be utterly exhausted at the end of your journey.
- Take a book into the hotel restaurant so that you can occupy yourself while you are being stared at by other diners.
- Getting home from holiday with a car full of suitcases and tired children is one of the most depressing things imaginable. If you cannot face unpacking and washing all your clothes, then get the children and souvenirs out of the car, put the suitcases on the ground and set them alight. Alternatively, get the children out of the car, put the kettle on and leave the unpacking until you've had a cup of tea and a chocolate Hob Nob.

23

things that go bump . . .

I cannot talk about death without mentioning what comes after it. Every religion has a differing view on the afterlife, and if you are an agnostic, the chances are that you believe that death ends in nothingness. I am not going to try to force my beliefs on anybody; all I want to do is tell you of my experiences and let you make up your own mind.

> My own belief has nothing to do with religion, but more to do with faith in the bond between two people. I believe that if two people love each other, and share a deep, emotional bond, that bond cannot be broken, even by death.

I know that by saying this I may be upsetting the people who believe that death is final and absolute, but too many things have happened to me since Charlie's death for me to believe otherwise.

Of course, my experiences could be written off as the delusional ramblings of a traumatised widow, but I'm not just talking about flickering lights and changes in temperature. I'm talking about feelings and premonitions; about dreams and waking manifestations.

I live in a fairly large house, and I used to feel edgy and scared when Charlie had to go away on business – I think most women feel nervous when their husband is away for the night. But since Charlie's death I have never felt uneasy at the thought of being alone in the house. I can walk around at night quite happily because I feel like Charlie is right there, by my side. I don't think of him as being away somewhere. I don't think of him as a mouldering body in a coffin. I think of him as my guide and protector.

It is your choice whether you believe that your partner has gone from you forever, or whether you choose to think as I do. I have experienced too much to believe that the end of life means the end of a person's existence. When Charlie died I was an emotional wreck, and at times I thought I might not have the strength to carry on. It was during such times that I would find myself getting a bit of help . . .

I would lie awake, exhausted, but too wired to sleep, and on several such occasions I became aware of a presence around me. I'm not talking about a ghost, but about a feeling in the air – a charge, an intensity. It was then that I would experience a surge in energy. I felt like I was being charged up, just like a battery. I could feel some kind of force flowing into my body, but it didn't scare me at all. I knew it was helping me. And in the morning, I felt peaceful and calm and better able to cope. Just when I had been at my weakest, I had been given a boost. I have no explanation for what happened to me; all I know is that it happened when I was at my lowest ebb and that it stopped when I became stronger. I thought, until recently, that I wouldn't be party to any more inexplicable occurrences, but I was wrong . . .

A couple of months ago I was lying on the spare bed while my two children took a bath in the room next door. I felt quite weary; it was the end of a long day and I decided to close my eyes for a minute. After a short while a strange feeling came over me and I became aware of some sort of presence around me – not of a single being, just a strange but very peaceful and benevolent atmosphere. My eyes were still shut, but had begun to flicker uncontrollably. I began to feel gentle pressure being exerted on my arms and legs, and I knew I couldn't have moved them, even if I had wanted to. At the same time I was being lifted up; I felt like I could rise up and float around the room, were it not for the pressure that was pushing me down onto the bed. My breathing slowed down and became shallow to such an extent that I was barely taking any breaths at all – I didn't feel like I needed the air; it all seemed rather irrelevant.

This lasted only for a matter of minutes – I could hear my daughters in the next room while it was happening and I didn't feel frightened or perturbed in any way. Gradually, the pressure eased off, and in doing so my arms began to lift up from the bed, quite of their own accord – in the same way that they will lift if you stand in a doorway and press outwards on the door frame for a while, and then walk forwards. I did feel a little strange, lying there with my arms in the air, but then I gradually felt the presence – or whatever it was – dissipating, and my arms came back to rest on the bed.

I'm not sure what I experienced, or why it happened when it did, but I do know that I'm not a fruitcake. What the loss of my husband has taught me is that death is not final and that there are things we cannot understand or even begin to explain in any rational way – we just have to accept them.

There have been countless occasions of flickering lights, loud bangs and sudden chills. I have grown more attuned to and more trusting of my intuition, and I know now to take notice when I have a premonition or a bad feeling about a certain event. I believe that Charlie is still around. It helps me to think this, and it helps my daughters. They know that they are special, because even though they don't have a daddy, they do have a guardian angel, and they are comforted when they go to bed at night by the knowledge that their father is watching over them as they sleep.

You can choose to ignore that voice in your head and to take no notice of your intuition, but would it hurt to let yourself be open to the faint possibility that death is not final? Would it hurt you to believe that the person you loved so very deeply is still around to give you love and guidance? Opening yourself up to the possibility that your partner may well be giving you messages and signs from the grave doesn't mean you are going to start seeing ghostly manifestations at the end of your bed each night, or hear strange moaning voices coming from the bathroom, saying 'Put the loo seat down.'

I've never seen a ghost, and I never want to, but I am comforted by the belief that I'm being watched over. I'm comforted by the feeling that I'm being looked after, and that when I need advice I only have to ask, and in one way or another I'll get the answer. It may well be a figment of my imagination, but as long as it's not hurting anybody, then who cares?

Believe what you like. The choice is yours.

24

resolution

Happiness. Joy. Acceptance. All words I have bandied around like there is some certainty that you will feel any of them again.

And do you feel any of them?

No? Well, let me tell you, I can absolutely guarantee that you will.

Now let me tell you why.

Imagine your life as an hourglass. Imagine the grains of sand as your store of hope, joy and love. The hourglass was full of your shared experiences and was brimming with happiness. When your partner died, your world inverted. Death – that black, desolate vortex – overwhelmed you. It turned your life upside down, leaving an empty vacuum. And in an instant, those grains of sand that constituted your former, happy self seemed such a long way off.

But what left you will eventually return.

Only regret will stop your recovery. Regret is such an empty emotion. It empties us of our hope and of our faith in the future.

Living your life as one of regret is like sticking your finger in the neck of an hourglass. You will stop all of the hope, the love and the trust returning to your life. You will stay in an empty vacuum.

I remember that feeling, that hateful, sucking emptiness. I remember wondering how I was ever going to cope with bringing my daughters up single-handed. I remember being stung by regret each time I thought of all the things Charlie wouldn't get to see.

And I remember the pain.

The pain I felt when a letter arrived on my doorstep addressed to Mr Charles Boydell; the pain I felt as I hurried out of the men's clothing department of Marks and Spencer, dropping socks that I had absent-mindedly picked up for my dead husband. I remember the pain and the envy, the longing and the bitterness – but I no longer feel any of those things. They have passed from my life like the grains of sand slipping through the neck of an hourglass. Light now illuminates a world that was once black and hopeless. Laughter substitutes tears, and hope replaces regret. There is nothing special about my recovery. All I did was allow time for the grief to leave me, and allow space for the joy to return. It didn't come gushing back into my life, but slowly trickled in as the grief began to subside. And what was emptiness is now a life lived to the full.

What I am trying to say in all this is that you cannot have both together.

> You cannot have hope until the despair has left you; you cannot feel love until you have stopped feeling hate. You may well become impatient for change and for recovery, but the greater your loss, the longer it will take for you to grieve.

Your life should not be lived in regret. You have so much to be proud of – just look how far you've come . . .

~

The following testimonials have all been written by widows and widowers.

Carolyn Roberts:

When my husband died suddenly and seemingly violently two weeks before Christmas in front of myself and my two teenage children, I veered between a numbed, almost daydream existence and one of utter hopelessness and despair. Having known him since I was 16 and been married for 28 years, I felt my life had come to an end. The funeral came and went and I sailed through it all calmly and controlled. People commented on how well I coped. When everyone went home and my children and I were left alone, I felt lost, with no one to talk to and no idea of what I was going to do . . .

My children watched me like a hawk. They wouldn't both go out at the same time as they thought I would be lonely. I pleaded that I was fine and that they needed to carry on with their lives – at 15 and 17 they had a lot of living to do. I decided that I had to get a social life outside what I had been used to. I was fed up with the same Friday night routine of going out with the two couples my husband and I had socialised with.

I posted my details on an Internet dating agency, but didn't have the courage to join. Two weeks later I received an e-mail from Ken. We had so much in common it was eerie. He too had been widowed. We met at a blues night, and a few months later he proposed. We married in September 2002 and life is great again.

There is life after death!

Jennie Leyden:

Reality hits like a sledgehammer. I am on my own. My beloved husband of 14 years has died, suddenly and unexpectedly. What do I do? Where do I go? Who should I speak to? Ring various organisations; speak to my GP? Do my children need counselling? Do I need counselling? Advice from friends and family – none of it helps fill the empty hole and none of it takes away the numbness. Children need me. They feed off me. I reassure them we can get through this, we will get through this, Dad would want us to. Months later I read an article and find the merrywidow website – eureka – exactly what I need. E-mail Kate:

> *'What can I say, absolutely marvellous. My husband died last year. We have two kids – Robert, ten, and Rachel, six. Yours is the first site and reference point that actually makes me feel normal. I have laughed and I have cried at your words, but more importantly I have empathised – I have screamed at the computer – yes, I did that! Yes, I thought that! Yes, I want that! Thank you.'*

My life has changed. I realise that I am not the only one – shit happens. I will be 40 this year; life will begin again for my children and me. I have met a lovely man who makes me so very happy. He is kind and he is patient; he could have been hand-picked for me – maybe he was? Stranger things have happened ...

Tony R:

So how does it get better? Obviously it doesn't, it only gets different. But the other night, watching a documentary as a couple bickered their way through an airport, I found myself laughing as well as crying. I remembered the arguments we sometimes had in the heat of getting through an airport somewhere in the Far East. It's almost three years now and the emotional scar tissue still shifts from time to time.

Managing to get around with the emotional equivalent of several missing limbs seems to be a trick one can learn. Finding ways to enjoy it is more difficult. Of course there is plenty of advice around, and I'd say you need to read or listen to lots of it and reject most of it.

Importantly it was on Kate's site I saw the first 'reasons to be cheerful' that I found at all believable. Twelve months further on I have found a few of my own. Helping people who seek out my support and advice has been rewarding, though so far the delight of a relationship and sex is still missing. For me, year one was rage, year two was confusion and now I seem to be a middle-aged adolescent combining both. Progress? Well, it is for me.

This is not what I wanted to do. It was 18 months after my wife's death before I could even start to laugh a little. Now whatever I do, I'm doing it on my terms, and sometimes with people I like and who like me.

Good luck if you are trying the same thing too.

Ann Nevard:

If anyone had said to me a year ago that I would smile again, that I would find the strength to go forward and face each new day, I would never have believed them. But I have emerged from the fog of bereavement. I've changed though. I'm not the same person I was before Tony died. I'm a new person. Every day I learn something new about myself – what I like and what I don't like. Being responsible for myself is scary too. Some days I cope better than others. If things break down, so do I, but I pick up the phone and speak to one of my sons, and with their support I get it sorted.

In the beginning I shared all my 'firsts' with absolutely everybody. The first time I put air in the tyres, the first time I used the hammer or screwdriver, the first time I went through the car wash. I was always on the phone! I was so proud of myself. I still am, of course, but I don't need to tell everyone any more.

You have to go through the healing process at your own pace. You can't hurry it. So don't compare yourself with someone else. And while life will never be the same again, that doesn't mean it has to be bad – just different.

Richard Martin:

An Australian friend once said: 'For you to move on you've got to rediscover the real you, not the person who has been married for 31 years.' Initially I didn't really understand what he was on about. I then realised that, to achieve a successful marriage, both parties go through a long process of compromise and, gradually, there is a blending of the two personalities. It's only when your partner dies that you realise how significantly that has affected the way you think and act. You then have to get used to being you again, a truly weird process, particularly at 52!

Every situation is unique and everyone reacts slightly differently, but in my case a numbed detachment led to a feeling of disbelief and panic, and a conviction that I'd never be happy again. However, I'm a pretty positive person and quite quickly began to take the 'sod it' attitude that this wasn't going to defeat me. Subsequently I've been able to rebuild my life into something that is starting to feel worthwhile again.

Sarah Snaydon:

Widow – the very word conjures images of thin-lipped, elderly matrons swathed in black; it can't mean vital, young or middle-aged women with so much to look forward to in the future.

Accepting that you are indeed a widow is only one of the many appalling changes a newly bereaved woman has to adapt to. At the stroke of a legal pen, you are suddenly single again. Everything is turned upside down, and your comfortable certainties are as out of reach as your wonderful husband. How on earth does anybody in this position ever smile again?

Sometimes, when the umpteenth person phones me up from a call centre and asks to speak to my husband, I find myself saying, 'Well, you'll have a job . . .' and then wondering what on earth gives me the capacity to find humour (albeit morbid) in such a bleak situation. The answer is that I am stronger than I ever thought I could be. A newly-widowed woman has to find Herculean resources of mental and emotional strength, and she also has to fill in tax returns, mow lawns and provide enough love for two parents. Nine months into my widowhood I frequently have moments when I feel totally desolate and very lonely. However, I also feel amazed at my capacity for coping, and that sustains me and makes me believe that, possibly, there will be some light – sometime.

They say that the greater the love, the greater the pain; but love endures – and the memories of that love will endure too. There are a lot of us about – we are not the only ones with this dreadful cross to bear, nor are we unable to carry it.

Harriet Knight:

My husband died on New Year's Day on our honeymoon in Costa Rica. We met when I was 18 and we were together for ten-and-a-half years. It goes without saying that this was the most awful thing that could possibly have happened, something I could never have imagined in my darkest dreams. But a year-and-a-half on, I am still here, without him. I am a changed person now, with a pretty simple outlook on life – I am just very, very grateful to be alive. And I now realise how important people are over material gains of any sort.

I could not have kept going without the consistent help from a great family and amazing friends – making me laugh, inviting me to do things with them, and taking the initiative to help without me having to ask them first. One of the most crucial survival tactics for me in the past year-and-a-half has been having regular short holidays, away from home and out of the country. This means getting away from the endless associations of my old life, which are around every corner in London.

I still see a counsellor, do Alexander technique, go to the gym and practise yoga to try and keep sane, and am thankful not to have been prescribed any mood-altering pills. The best bit of advice came from my doctor, who told me to exercise at least two or three times a week as it staves off depression. And she was right. I think I've survived it, and apart from the odd bad day when I retreat to bed and watch trashy TV, my new life is going just fine.

Gill Woodman:

I lost my husband, aged 45, 10 months ago – 10 months next Thursday to be exact – and I miss him desperately every day. But I know he is with me and I know he would be telling me to get on with my life – he knows I will never forget him. And I am trying. Already I am doing things I would never have done had he still been here. In November I will be doing the New York Marathon – as he should have done just four weeks after his death. I'll be raising money for the same charity and he'll be with me every step of the way, shaking his head in wonderment at my efforts. I should point out that I am not brave enough to run it – nor would my knees take such punishment – but I am assured by the people at Get Kids Going! (the charity for which I am raising money) that power walking it is just as acceptable. It will take me at least six-and-a-half hours but I really don't care. The thought of going there and taking part in my one and only marathon is what has kept me going so far during this first, extremely difficult year.

I've done other things too, like learning to salsa and how to give facials. And I know I am becoming a stronger person than I was – partly out of necessity as Rich is no longer there to hold my hand through all that life throws my way – but also because I want to be. I want to prove to someone – God? I don't know – that I can survive this tragedy. And I need to do it for my children too, to show them that there can be a future, albeit not the one we had envisaged less than a year ago.

David Robarts:

If someone had said to me 17 months ago that life would return to something approaching normality by now I would have laughed in their faces (actually I would probably have told them to fuck off, what do you know!). Astonishingly, I can honestly say that we have journeyed through the worst of our bereavement, and that normality – albeit of a weird variety – is our reward.

My wife died in October 2002, after a six-month sojourn in hospital, leaving me with four young children to raise. My grief was of a depth that dominated everything and, with the benefit of hindsight, I am sure I was clinically depressed for at least the first six months.

Two things carried me through the first year. First, the wife of a man who suffered from the same disease as my wife wrote on their website something along the lines of 'You wouldn't wish this on anyone but as we don't have a choice in going through it all, the choice is in how you choose to deal with it.' Second, I was very lucky – or was it fate? – to hear Kate being interviewed on Five Live *shortly after Titania died. A chord was struck in my brain and I visited the merrywidow site. I read through the entire site in one sitting and have since frequently returned.*

The message from most other sites I have visited strikes me as encouraging self-pity and wallowing in professional widowerism. Everyone goes through the same emotional steps during the bereavement process but it seems that many people get to a certain stage and stop. I lost count of the number of widows/widowers who told me that the second year would be worse than the first – well bugger me, here I am six months into the second year and it's fine!

Yes, it has been difficult getting here and no, it is not all a bed of roses (getting unexpectedly upset by Casualty *or, worse,* Coronation Street *is a nightmare!). But once you learn not to do the 'what ifs?' and accept that you are guilty of nothing more than having loved your partner, you can move on. That's simplistic but essentially true. I remember the day last summer when I was mowing and suddenly realised I was content – the guilt that engendered! I am now having the most vivid dreams of her and I wake up with a smile, feeling great and no longer in floods of tears – what a relief.*

The bottom line for me now, and the way I dealt with the loss of my 38-year-old soul mate, is that (as it says elsewhere in these testimonials) shit happens and all we can do is get a mop out and clean up the subsequent mess. It's not nice but if you've had children you know you can do it! My advice, for what it's worth, is elect to cope and reconnect with life – happiness is a much nicer place than sadness.

~

You will have experienced the best and worst that human nature has to offer. You will have learned to recognise what is good in people, and to see right through those who do not have your best interests at heart. You will have discovered the true nature of friendship, and will understand and value those who remained true to you when you were at your lowest ebb. You will become a kinder person and a better friend. You will become noble and wise. People will seek you out. Friends will come to you with their problems, and you will help them, because benevolence is borne out of personal loss. You will see other people's petty and inconsequential problems for what they are, but you will do everything in your power to aid those people who are truly in need of your help. Your insight into the human psyche is something most psychiatrists would gladly sell their couch for. It is all within you – others can see it; all you have to do is recognise that it is there.

Acknowledge your power. Acknowledge your experience of death and your ability to recover from it. Understand the fundamental changes that have taken place within you since you lost your partner, and go forward. Go forward and make a new life. Go forward and find happiness.

If you have children, they should grow up into strong and resolute adults. They will value your love and have pride in their family. Theirs will not be an easy life, but they will have clarity of vision and knowledge of the world far beyond that of their peers. Death will have given your children the strength to go though life with their heads held high, and as long as they are secure in your love, your children will be able to face anything fate can throw at them in the future.

Being a single parent can be a difficult and thankless job at times, but the benefits can far outweigh the minus points. When people say that my children are a real credit to me, I feel that everything I have had to go though has been worthwhile. I feel pride in the knowledge that I've done a good job in bringing them up by myself, and I know that Charlie would be proud of me too. I can forget all the shouting, the rage and the tears. I can forgive myself the times when I felt like leaving them. I can forgive myself because I know it was grief that made me act so irrationally, and I have left that grief behind.

You may well have learned new skills since the death of your partner. Your cooking has probably improved, especially if you have children, because not only do you have to cook for them, you now understand just how hard it is to nip off to the local Indian takeaway whenever the mood takes you. Cooking may be a chore, or you may love it, but one thing is certain: you will have had to learn to do it on a regular basis. Cooking is about showing love, and cooking for your children will reinforce their security and their pride in you. Beans on toast may be the best you ever come up with, but to your child it will be like eating ambrosia.

If you have started to tackle jobs around the house, then you will either be applying for a spot on *DIY SOS* and begging Lowri Turner to pay you a visit, or you will have completed a few essential jobs and will be feeling justifiable pride in the results. It will only take one successful DIY project to instigate a major shift in the way you feel about yourself, and if you get a taste for it, you will be amazed at the confidence it will instil. Cooking and DIY are not that dissimilar when you think about it. Making a cheese soufflé and wiring in a light fitting are both tasks that take a bit of practice, and both have the potential for disaster. But if you read the instructions carefully, have the right equipment and sufficient patience, then making a successful job of both is well within your grasp. Granted, you can't kill yourself with a cheese soufflé quite as easily as you can with a live wire, but I think you know what I mean.

If you are not confident enough to tackle home maintenance, then the chances are that at some stage you will have had to resort to using the services of a professional. That, in itself, can be quite an ordeal, especially if you've always relied on your partner to deal with tradesmen. But you will have had to do it, and regardless of whether it was a pleasant experience or an absolute nightmare, the very act of completing such an onerous task will have helped to restore some of your self-belief. In time you will become so steely and astute that the washing machine repairman will work himself up into a real lather when he knows he has to pay you a visit. You will develop a look, which says, 'Don't fuck with me – I've seen death and I'm not scared of anything now.' Give this look just before being presented with a bill and you might be genuinely surprised by the results.

The 'don't fuck with me' look has a number of other applications. You will be amazed at just how many situations require it, and you will be equally amazed at how empowered you begin to feel once you have mastered it. It will have replaced the 'please sedate me, I'm not right in the head' look; the 'don't look at me, I'm depressed and worthless' glance; and the full-on 'I've had enough of this. I want to die. My life is over and I'm going to top myself if you don't open another checkout' stare.

In the Vietnam War, the soldiers who were suffering from shell shock or battle fatigue had a look that was christened the 'thousand yard stare', so called because their gaze seemed locked on something way off in the distance. Such men were not just tired and demoralised; they were locked into a cycle of reliving all the horror they had witnessed as soldiers. A photographer for *Life* magazine captured an image of one such soldier, and by gazing at the image of that young man's eyes, it is possible to get a snapshot of all the misery, hardship and hopelessness he had suffered in the theatre of war. It is a stark and haunting image of mental illness, but perfectly illustrates that if a mind is made to lock away mental anguish, the eyes will still provide an open window. Madness can be disguised by all kinds of artifice: you can smile and laugh; you can make jokes and tell people you are coping really well with your life, but that look will betray you every time. Therefore, if you are really unsure as to whether you have grieved properly, just ask a friend to look into your eyes, and then ask, 'Do I look happy?' If the answer is a resounding 'No' then you are going to have to sit down and ask yourself 'Why?'

But don't despair. When you do start to look happy again, you will also feel stronger than ever before. It will have been a long and bloody battle, but once you have exorcised all of your personal demons, your look of madness will change into something altogether different. You will now have in your ocular arsenal a weapon so powerful that you will feel like a latter-day Medusa. Use it carefully, but know that what people see in your eyes is only your irrepressible self-belief and strength shining forth. And it will shine forth, and it will illuminate all those people who live petty, nit-picking lives, and make them see how closed and shallow they really are.

You will feel indestructible, inscrutable and omnipotent. You, yes you! Miserable, grieving person that you were – just look at yourself now. Look in the mirror and tell me that you don't feel kindly and benevolent. Look in the mirror and see a person who no longer hangs his head, who no longer lowers her eyes. Look in the mirror and see yourself anew; you're a battler, a survivor, an uncompromising 'I won't take no for an answer' bad-ass. Be proud of yourself. Be proud of your achievements. Widow or widower, once you've worn black you'll never look back.

I have developed a deeply philosophical nature since Charlie's death. I look at the world differently now. I have a relaxed attitude to life, and I no longer fear what fate has in store for me. I welcome each new challenge that life throws at me. I have a confidence that comes not from another person, or a bottle of pills, or a line of coke; my confidence comes from years spent looking within myself and trying to find the strength to go on. My confidence comes from building up a life that lay shattered into a solid and loving foundation for the future. Widowhood is a kind of retreat. It allows us to contemplate all the many facets of everyday life that others so often take for granted, and to learn to treasure them. It allows us the deepest introspection. Silence and solitude can be a blessing as well as a curse, and I am constantly amazed at how much more attuned I am, both to my own feelings and also to the feelings of others. Coming out of the grieving process is like walking out of a cave for the first time after months spent in darkness. The world seems brighter somehow.

I have come to a rational understanding of all the events that led up to Charlie's death and have forgiven myself all of the things that once plagued me with regret. The jumbled mass of thoughts and emotions that clouded my mind in the first year after Charlie's death has now cleared. I have a thousand yard stare, but not one that reflects my anguish. It is a kind of second sight. I now see through what others get bogged down by; I see solutions to complex emotional issues. I see right into other people's hearts, because I have looked so deeply into my own.

Introspection is a wonderful thing

~

The one question that still vexes me, six years after Charlie's death, is this: 'When am I going to meet a man?' It is an irritant to me; it flares up like a nasty boil and often at the most inconvenient of times. I've tried the gym, solo holidays and Internet dating. I have exhausted all the suggestions thought up by helpful friends, and to no avail. But always, when I think I'm going to spend the rest of my life alone, I am struck by the thought that perhaps there is a good reason for my being single. Many people have suggested that I should consider a one-night stand, but I always tell them that once I got started, I would find it very hard to stop. My friends have concerns for the well-being of any potential suitors, on health and safety grounds; and I have a doctor friend who is anxious to offer a full medical to any man who might consider taking me on. But I know when the time is right all things will come to me. It is part of my philosophical nature. I understand that everything happens for a reason, and that if I haven't met a man up to now, then it is because I still have more to do. But oh, the joy when I do.

Losing a partner is a devastating blow, but if you can pick yourself up from it you will have so much to look forward to. Imagine the joy when you do eventually find somebody to love again. Imagine the pleasure of your first kiss. Imagine the sexual frisson of going out on your first proper date. You will be as flustered and nervous as a skittish teenager, a born-again virgin. A novice. But think of how wonderful it will be to fall in love again. You have a second chance to make somebody happy, a second chance to give love and to be loved in return. And you can do so, not with the knotted, suppressed bitterness of a divorcée, but with a clear and open heart.

Yes, you have scars; yes, you have memories, but now you must look to the future, to your future happiness, and to that of another person. Live your life for the moment rather than clinging on to the past. Look back fondly on the love you have lost, but accept that your life did not end when your partner died. Live your life. Live it now. The future is yours. Happiness will be yours, and nobody deserves it more than you.

resources

British Association for Counselling and Psychotherapy (BACP)
1 Regent Place
Rugby
Warwickshire CV21 2PJ
Tel: 01788 578328/9
Website: www.counselling.co.uk

Will provide details of counselling organisations and services in your local area

The Child Bereavement Trust
Aston House
West Wycombe, High Wycombe
Buckinghamshire HP14 3AG
Tel: 01494 446648
Fax: 01494 440057
E-mail: jthomas@thecbt.freeserve.co.uk
Website: www.childbereavement.org

The Child Bereavement Trust provides support and counselling for grieving families. It is a charity that cares for bereaved families by training and supporting professional carers. Established in 1994 by Jenni Thomas and Julia Samuel, it aims to increase awareness and acknowledge the importance of grief and loss.

It offers a number of helpful books and videos for grieving

families as well as professionals. There is also an information and support line for professionals caring for bereaved families. It is available on 0845 357 1000 between 9am and 5pm.

Citizens Advice Bureau

Myddelton House
115–123 Pentonville Road
London N1 9LZ

Contact head office or look in your local phone book for your nearest branch for free, impartial and confidential advice about death, bereavement and financial matters.

Cruse Bereavement Care

Cruse House
126 Sheen Road
Richmond
Surrey TW9 1UR
Day-by-Day Helpline: 0870 167 1677
E-mail Helpline: helpline@crusebereavementcare.org.uk
General E-mail: info@crusebereavementcare.org.uk
Website: www.crusebereavementcare.org.uk

Cruse Bereavement Care exists to promote the well-being of bereaved people and to enable anyone suffering a bereavement caused by death to understand their grief and cope with their loss.

Cruse is now the largest bereavement counselling charity in the world and has nearly 200 branches throughout the UK and will provide a contact number for a local branch. It offers confidential counselling and support and can also offer advice on practical matters. The mail order service offers more than 100 books, booklets and pamphlets designed to help the bereaved and those who support them.

Memorials By Artists
Memorials by Artists Ltd
Snape Priory
Snape
Suffolk IP17 1SA
Contact: Harriet Frazer or Hilary Meynell
Tel: 01728 688934
E-mail: harriet@memorialsbyartists.co.uk

National Association of Bereavement Services
20 Norton Folgate
London E1 6DB
Tel (referrals): 020 7247 1080
Tel (admin): 020 7247 0617

Information about bereavement counselling services in your local area.

National Association of Memorial Masons
27a Albert Street
Rugby
Warwickshire CV21 2SG
Tel: 01788 542264
Fax: 01788 542276
E-mail: enquiries@namm.org.uk
Website: www.namm.org.uk

List of members who can create individual memorials and operates a code of practice for members.

National Association of Widows
54-57 Allison Street
Digbeth
Birmingham B5 5TH
Tel: 0121 643 8348

Information and details of local branches. A contact list for young widows is also available.

The Samaritans
PO Box 9090
Stirling FK8 2SA
National number: 0345 909090
E-mail: jo@smaritans.org or samaritans@anon.twwells.com
Website: www.samaritans.org.uk

The primary aim of The Samaritans is to be available at any hour of the day or night to befriend people who are facing a personal crisis, including bereavement. Sometimes it is better to talk in confidence to someone with time to listen, who is not a close friend or family member. Also see your local phone book.

UK Council for Psychotherapy (UKCP)
167-169 Great Portland Street
London W1W 5PF
Tel: 020 7436 3002
Fax: 020 7436 3013
E-mail: ukcp@psychotherapy.org.uk
Website: www.psychotherapy.org.uk

The Way Foundation
PO Box 74
Penarth CF64 5ZD
Tel: 02920 711209
E-mail: info@wayfoundation.org.uk
Website: www.wayfoundation.org.uk

Support charity with networking groups and social events for those bereaved under the age of 50.

Winston's Wish
Clara Burgess Centre
Bayshill Road
Cheltenham GL50 3AW
Family line: 0845 20 30 40 5
Website: www.winstonswish.org.uk

A fantastic site supporting bereaved children and young people. My own children love it.

www.ifishoulddie.co.uk
Kate Burchill created this invaluable site after the death of her father. It is an excellent general information site that is not linked to any particular religion or philosophy. It is packed with essential information and I can't recommend it highly enough.

index